"This book is *not* a how-to book, _____ \d it challenges Christian educators to ponde_ _____ ` on their call to teaching. As I devoured the bo _____ es: those containing both chocolate and pea _____ ___ butter alone are great, but together they create a ne _____ ___ the same way, there are many books sharing philosophies of education from classroom management to curriculum. There is also a plethora of self-help books on growing your relationship with the Lord. Donovan Graham has melded two such books together, and he encourages educators to think through how they 'do education Christianly.' This book overcomes the secular/sacred dualism that has weakened our public education system, making this a must-read for all Christian educators called to serve in the public schools. The concepts shared are truly transformational."

—Finn Laursen, Executive Director
Christian Educators Association International, Westlake, Ohio

"Donovan Graham writes another foundational text—a *Teaching Redemptively* for public school teachers. Graham develops a Scripture-based blueprint that guides the reader toward redemptive teaching, focusing on calling, image bearing, and grace. He captures the reality of the classroom (students and teachers) in a fallen world and lays out how teachers can most effectively represent Christ through their actions and the creation of a safe and caring classroom community. Graham writes of teacher decision making including curriculum choices, learning activities, grading, and discipline approaches through the framework of grace using Scripture and prayer as the required foundation. He then guides the reader to become dedicated to a relationship with Christ, developing a 'rhythm for living' and partnering with other Christian teachers in a collaborative effort to teach with excellence and do all to glorify the Father."

—Dr. Yvonne Trotter, Assistant Professor of Education at Geneva College
and CEAI Ohio State Director, Beaver Falls, Pennsylvania

"Dr. Graham gets to the heart of the matter in a way that is both gently gracious but dauntingly challenging for Christians in the public sector. A must-read for image-bearing educators working with image-bearing people! This book parallels God's way of dealing with all of us as broken image bearers: one hand pointing with exhortation to pursue others with love and grace while the other arm is around us, giving us the fullness of His love and confidence to go forth! *Making a Difference* gives Christians in the public sector reason to grow in our own faith and also glorious potential with both students and staff. Sewn together by the threads of grace, this book is a catalyst for making change agents in the world and for transforming how Christians view the public school system."

—Rebecca Anne Groves, Sixth-Grade Teacher and Professional Development Coordinator
Hoech Middle School, Ritenour School District, St. Louis, Missouri

"In this book, Donovan Graham challenges educators to act in accordance with the foundational truth that God created human beings in His image. He illustrates ways in which this truth, taken to heart and applied to educators and students alike, can transform relationships at every level in schools. This book extends his vision to the public school setting, building on the foundation laid in his earlier book for Christian school settings, *Teaching Redemptively*. And Donovan Graham is one of those rare educators whose own character and practice thoroughly exemplify and embody the advice he gives to others. I know from working alongside him that he amply incarnates the grace-filled practice that he advocates here."

—Dr. Daphne Wharton Haddad, Professor of Education and former colleague of Dr. Graham
Covenant College, Lookout Mountain, Georgia

"As a Christian public school teacher, I clearly see the dark clouds that threaten our effectiveness in living out the image of God in our teaching: standardized test scores, pacing and curriculum guides, and an overall reductionist approach in regard to students. Dr. Graham's newest book encourages and challenges us that we must never forget that our calling is more than getting good test scores from our students. Our calling is to live out the gospel and present to our students the grace of the living and true God, even in the midst of public education."

—Christian Clark
Hixson Elementary School, Hixson, Tennessee

"The strength of this book is that it charts a course for how Christians who are teaching in public schools can do so in ways that reflect the gospel of grace without reducing the complexity of our calling. This book is realistic and biblical. It asks and answers the questions that thoughtful Christian public school teachers want to know and provides a framework for faithfulness. Highly recommended!"

—Mark Redfern, Sixth-Grade Social Studies Teacher
Burns Middle School, Owensboro, Kentucky

"*Making a Difference: Christian Educators in Public Schools* is a real treasure for public school educators. It is a much-needed resource with spiritual direction and practical applications. I longed for such a resource throughout my thirty years as an educator. Now it is here! Thank you, Dr. Graham!"

—Dr. Lisa D. Murley, Assistant Professor of Teacher Education
Western Kentucky University, Bowling Green, Kentucky

Making a Difference

Making a Difference:

Christian Educators in Public Schools

DONOVAN L. GRAHAM

Purposeful Design Publications
Colorado Springs, Colorado

Purposeful Design Publications is the publishing division of the Association of Christian Schools International (ACSI) and is committed to the ministry of Christian school education, to enable Christian educators and schools worldwide to effectively prepare students for life. As the publisher of textbooks, trade books, and other educational resources within ACSI, Purposeful Design Publications strives to produce biblically sound materials that reflect Christian scholarship and stewardship and that address the identified needs of Christian schools around the world.

Printed in the United States of America

18 17 16 15 14 13 12 11   1 2 3 4 5 6 7

Graham, Donovan L.
  Making a Difference: Christian Educators in Public Schools
  ISBN 978-1-58331-387-9 Catalog #6495

Designer: Michael Riester
Editorial team: Gina Brandon, John Conaway
Cover image: ThinkStock.com

Purposeful Design Publications
A Division of ACSI
PO Box 65130 • Colorado Springs, CO 80962-5130
Customer Service: 800-367-0798 • www.acsi.org

To my wife, Wilma,
whose continual sacrifice for me is a picture of Jesus,
and all the teachers who sacrifice themselves
to be a picture of Jesus to their students.

Contents

Preface

As I have long considered the biblical principles that should inform and shape our educational process, I have been convinced all along that such principles are universal and that they apply to all learning situations—schools, homes, churches, and any other organizations that have a role in and a responsibility for educating people. While teaching at Covenant College, I asked my students to come to firm convictions concerning their beliefs about such principles, let those convictions always direct them, and then determine how to apply them in the circumstances in which they found themselves. Such would probably not be an issue except for the fact that in our country there is definite resistance to the inclusion of the Christian religion in schools.

We do not have to lay our Christian convictions aside to teach or to be administrators in such environments. While we may be legally restricted in what we may *say* in the public school classroom, there is no such restriction on what we *do* in the educational process that flows out of those biblical principles about the learner, the teacher, learning, the curriculum, and the relationship between teacher and student. One of my deepest convictions is that the educational *process* teaches much more than what we *say*. Therefore, we can make the grace of the gospel be the foundation for our processes in designing curricular experiences, in learning tasks and activities, in measuring learning, and certainly in dealing with our students in personal ways. Thus, the gospel is infused into the ethos of our classrooms.

In my earlier effort to put my convictions about education into writing, *Teaching Redemptively: Bringing Grace and Truth into Your Classroom*, I set forth what I believe to be biblical principles that should guide and shape our educational processes. Because the challenge in that book was directed more toward teachers in Christian schools, I was asked by some who work with Christian teachers in public schools to write a version that was directed more to the context in which they work. This book is the result.

Again, because I believe many of the principles are valid regardless of the context, there are ideas from the earlier book that show up again in this second book. There are some emphases though, especially in regard to the *relationship* question and concerning the *teacher's need for intimacy with God,* that are new. The stories come essentially from teachers who work in public schools and also from my own experience. I trust they will provide the context for considering the application of these ideas to the classroom.

Throughout this book, *the foundational emphasis is on creating an atmosphere of grace in the classroom and treating students as the image bearers of God that He created them to be.* For lives to be changed, the grace of the gospel must be the air that they breathe, and the students must be viewed through the lens of who they really are—image bearers of God. To do so is to be a living reflection of Jesus through the relationship that develops between teacher and student.

Donovan L. Graham
May 2011

Acknowledgments

While I have always felt that the principles and practices described in my earlier book, *Teaching Redemptively: Bringing Grace and Truth into Your Classroom*, could be applied in any school circumstances, I owe this current attempt to contextualize those principles for the many Christian teachers in non-Christian school settings to Dr. Vernard Gant, director of Urban School Services for the Association of Christian Schools International (ACSI). Dr. Gant's passion in life is to reach and serve the more than 20 million children in our nation who live in poverty and attend very under-resourced schools (Snyder and Dillow 2011, 81). To that end, ACSI, though an organization primarily serving Christian schools, has accepted his challenge to also reach out to Christian teachers in all types of schools in order to give these children some opportunity for hope. It is a bold and very commendable step on the part of those at ACSI.

Early in the process, another key person joined the discussion on the need for such a book as this—Finn Laursen, executive director of the Christian Educators Association International (CEAI), an organization that exists to support and encourage Christian teachers in public schools. His immediate and continuing enthusiasm for this project has been an encouragement and a challenge, matching that of Dr. Gant.

Were it not for the encouragement and enthusiasm of these two men, I doubt I would have pursued this book. But there is also a third person who played a key role in this project through his cooperation, willingness, assistance, and ability to get things done—Steve Babbitt, assistant vice president, Purposeful Design Publications, at ACSI. Steve has been not only a great publisher but also a great friend. How nice to have the publisher on your side rather than harassing you!

Publishers are very important people in book writing, but so are editors. I have been privileged again to have had this work edited by Gina Brandon at ACSI. What a gem at wordsmithing she is! I could never catch the mistakes and omissions she has caught, and it is always wonderful to have someone make your thoughts understandable. Her suggestions are all to the reader's benefit.

And then there is my faithful wife, Wilma, who not only believes in me but finds all the ways she can to help me with such a project. She has spent hours transcribing teacher interviews, hours reading and proofing with me, and hours alone while I sat at a keyboard. She has been my constant encouragement to keep on even when I did not feel like it.

Finally, I want to thank the teachers who were willing to give me the stories that appear in this book. All of them gave me an idea of the challenges that some of their students face but also some of the things they have found that have made a difference in those students' lives. Over and over again, my thoughts about treating children as image bearers in an atmosphere of grace were corroborated by the stories from these teachers. Without their help this could have all sounded theoretical, but their stories are grounded in real experience.

Introduction

Teaching is an arduous, challenging, sometimes rewarding, and sometimes frustrating task under any circumstances. But attempting to teach from faith beliefs as a Christian in a setting that openly, and sometimes angrily, seeks to prevent one from doing so makes matters much worse. Teaching in places where students come from broken, uncaring, and frightening environments, where at worst their very lives may at times be threatened and at best there is little or no support for them, multiplies the difficulty even more. Those who teach in such settings have an enormous task, and they are always at risk of either burning out or turning cold and mechanical just to survive.

What would it take for teachers to not only survive but even thrive in such circumstances? What would it take for them to know a sense of calling and to have the power to faithfully pursue it? How might they reflect their faith in the classroom without crossing legal boundaries designed to restrict them? How would such teachers hope to make a difference in students' lives when so many forces are against them?

To make a difference in students' lives, we have to realize that just as with Jesus, lives are changed through *relationship*. Again, as with Jesus, such relationships are built on *grace*. The big act of grace is to treat students as *image bearers of God*—fallen, yes, but still image bearers. To do that we must receive that grace from Jesus ourselves and live out our calling as His image bearers as well. To maintain that flow of grace from God to us to our students requires an *intimate relationship with Him*. And finally, we must find or create a *community* that can support us and join us in pursuit of our calling. These are the five major themes I will try to explore in this book—relationship, grace, image bearing, intimacy with God, and community.

Theme 1: Relationships

God has existed in relationship since eternity. The members of the Trinity love, relate to, rely on, work with, and celebrate with one another. At the time of creation, God decided to spread the wonder of that relationship to humankind. It was so good that He wanted to share it. Thus, human beings were created to be in a loving relationship with the three members of the Godhead, and with one another. Relationship is at the very core of our existence.

It is no wonder, then, that meaning and value in life should come primarily through relationships. We learn through relationships as we watch and interact with others in new experiences. We experience joy as we laugh and celebrate together. We understand a good bit of who we are through our interactions with others—how they respond to us and we respond to them. We can accomplish a good deal on our own, but we accomplish much more in conjunction with others. The relationship that develops between us as we work or play together becomes something we desire more of because it is so satisfying.

When people are asked to look back at who or what transformed their lives, or at least had a great impact on them, do they often say it was a textbook? Was it a great curriculum design? Was it the new teaching techniques a teacher used? Or was it a fantastic new school building? No, they do not. Many will mention a teacher, but it will be the relationship they had with that teacher that affected them.

Thus, if we are serious enough about teaching to want to actually influence the lives of the children who populate our classrooms, we must first consider the relationship we seek to create with them. Life change will come about more through that which is personal than professional. Curriculum is important. Teaching to learning styles is important. Meaningful content is important. Success is important. But none of these things matches up to the one-to-one relationship that results from a teacher who truly loves a child.

If we want to change lives of broken students, we will have to be in a significant relationship with them. Our rigor, our resources, our money and facilities, and our latest approach to curriculum and instruction will not do it in themselves. Lives are seldom changed merely through verbal or written instruction.

Theme 2: Grace

Human relationships that have a transforming effect are patterned after the relationship in the Trinity. There is love, trust, dependence, confidence, humility—never a concern for power grabbing—joy in one another's being, and unity in purpose and desire. Of course one may ask, "How can that exist between fallen human beings?" There is only one means, and that is through *grace*. A relationship between a fallen teacher and a fallen student can only begin to resemble the divine relationship through receiving and giving grace.

When Jesus came to transform a fallen world, His means and method was grace. It was a very broken world with many messed-up people. Transforming the world came about through transforming individuals who would live differently in that world—individuals who would be filled with His grace and who would give it away to others.

It is significant to realize that His approach to change was deeply personal. He reached into the hearts of those who would respond to that grace and gave away Himself to them. He did not bring about change through some well-defined curriculum of truth; He spoke in parables. He did not have the latest teaching techniques; He told stories and asked questions. He did not have lots of slick and impressive resources; He used sticks, coins, fish, and sick children.

His curriculum was Himself; He said He was the truth. Broken people were made whole by trusting themselves to Him and His grace. When He explained something, He did it in a manner that meant something to the hearers personally.

None of these people deserved His time, attention, love, commitment, and certainly not His very life. That, however, is the nature of grace—we get the opposite of what we deserve.

If a teacher is to have a relationship with a student that transforms the life of that student, it must begin, and continue, with grace. Efforts to merely control, force compliance, or otherwise make students into something we can be proud of and be comfortable with will actually ruin relationships and reduce the likelihood of a positive impact on students.

Theme 3: Bearing the Image of God

In the Bible, the first thing, and the most important thing, we hear about human beings is that we were created in the image of God. We were not created to *be* God but to be a *living picture* of who He is. An image is not the real thing, but it represents the real thing. And while the entrance of sin into the creation marred that image, it was not destroyed. We cannot escape the image even if we try. We will always be active, purposeful, rational, creative, free, responsible, moral, and social beings. (This list does not complete the characteristics of God placed in us.)

The issue is what we do with that image—whether it is lived out according to God's character and purpose or whether it is lived out according to some other character and purpose. For instance, our rationality and creativity can be exercised to conserve life (through medicine) or to destroy life (again through medicine). Our freedom can be used to serve others (friendships with the poor), or it can be used to serve only ourselves (making money at the expense of those who have very little).

The challenge for those of us who want to be faithful to God and what He made us to be is to deal with fallen image bearers in a way that neither ignores the image nor the fallenness. Often our first reaction to a student who uses his creativity to disrupt the class is to crunch the creativity rather than redirect it, to stop the creativity rather than try to move it toward a good end.

An image marred and distorted and misdirected is still the image, however. We cannot treat it as otherwise. Thus, dealing with students as image bearers, albeit fallen image bearers, is one of the most fundamental concerns of our teaching. *Everything* is affected by using this as our starting point and keeping it as our driving perspective.

Recognizing ourselves as image bearers is equally important. There is much in the educational world that would like to reduce us to something less than what we are. Curriculum guides try to determine all that we teach and even sometimes how we teach. State proficiency tests have extraordinary power over what we teach—our success as teachers is determined by our students' scores, and now sometimes our salaries are determined by the same. Parents have expectations, school officials have expectations, and textbook publishers have means of enticing us to use their products by making everything so simple for us (for example, they produce everything for us).

One of the unknown (or at least unspoken) effects of these efforts to reduce us to something less than what we are is simply the emotional, mental, physical, and spiritual toll it takes on us to try to be something we are not. God made us in His image so that we might have life, not a mechanical, deathlike existence. To be treated as something less than an image bearer, or to act as something less, is to drain us of life—something that faces many, many teachers who work with children and who have never been treated like image bearers either.

Our calling is not to fill a job or pursue a profession; our calling is to embrace what bearing God's image is in our own unique way and to be willing and able to live faithfully to that calling. Our calling is to bring God glory by being alive in what He made us to be. Teachers, though fallen as well, are redeemed image bearers of God who are called to reveal the heart of Jesus and His kingdom in all they do.

Therefore, it is extremely important that our worldview, and way we approach life, has as one of its cornerstones that all human beings, students and teachers alike—redeemed or unredeemed, pleasant or a pain in the neck—must be seen and treated as image bearers of God.

Theme 4: Intimacy with God—Care of a Teacher's Soul

At the very core of a teacher's life is his or her soul. This is where all the dimensions of existence are centered or rooted. It is where one meets God; for that is where He dwells, and where we, in the most fundamental part of our existence, dwell as well. Christian teachers are often so committed, so willing to sacrifice, so gifted and called, so seemingly tireless that their own souls often go unattended. Though the shift is slow and subtle, it is all too easy to allow the King's work to replace the King Himself. We can love doing the King's work and not realize that our love for the King is waning. What a very successful plan for burnout! Clever, right? The enemy uses the joy of doing the King's work to separate us from the King. I suspect we could not find a single case of Christian burnout that would not somehow include a testimony to a loss in fellowship with, and growing distance from, our God who created us and loves us with no end.

When good teachers burn out, there is an obvious loss to the students as well as the huge loss to the teacher. However, there is also a great loss to God, and it is not just the loss of a warrior in the battle. His kingdom will reign whether we as individuals can stay in the battle or not. No, the great loss to God is *personal*. God is robbed of the personal relationship with each of those He longs to know and love. Did you get that—*longs* to know and love?

God created us for relationship with Him—*close* relationship. Oh yes, He has work for each of us to do as He invites us to join Him in His work, but that is not the primary reason for our existence. His greatest desire for us is that we know Him and love Him as He knows and loves us. Therefore, to drift away from Him because of the demands and exhaustion that characterize our lives is to cheat Him, not just us.

But it is also true that we cannot carry out our calling to be His image bearers in dealing with our broken students if we are not so connected to Him that His love and life sustain us. To try to extend grace to all broken students without a constant, daily infusion of His grace is almost akin to suicide. It takes great energy to treat others with grace, and it takes great surrender to accept it for ourselves. Unless we walk closely with Him, our souls will dry up, and we will either burn out or turn coldhearted and mechanical in order to survive.

Therefore, we must consider what it takes to walk with God in a way that keeps us alive and fresh and ready to give to our students what He gives to us.

Theme 5: We Can't Go It Alone

As teachers in public schools, we can often find ourselves feeling quite alone. A public school would not generally see the purpose for education in the same way we do. Not many teachers would adhere to the high view of students we have discussed.

The sense of calling to teaching is not likely to be as deep as ours either. In many public schools, there is the ever-present resistance to the person of Christ or His involvement with anything in life. And finally, there is such diversity in backgrounds and beliefs in the students that there is no common ground there either. The public school can be a lonely place for a Christian teacher.

God has not abandoned the public school though, and He certainly has not abandoned those children in the schools that He wants to claim for His own. Nor has He said that the public school is one institution where it does not matter if He has a witness to the King and the kingdom. Quite the contrary, the public school is perhaps one of the most "missional" fields in our society.

We note that Jesus, though alone as the God-man, did not move out into the world to reclaim it by Himself. He sought, and found, partners for His work. While they were far from perfect during His three-year mission on earth, they did support Him and one another. While they let Him down in significant times, He still trusted them with the most important work in the world. *He spent much time in solitude with His Father, much time in community with His disciples, and then much time in ministry among the broken people of the world.* (It may be worth noting that He did not necessarily spend much time trying to change the establishment. Instead, He focused on individuals and groups that needed Him and who sensed when He was present.)

There is little that feels worse than being alone when facing a difficult, seemingly unending, and often fruitless task. It takes a terrible toll. *Thus, it seems imperative that we consider ways and means that teachers of like mind, even if not in the same building, can lean on and support one another in this calling of changing lives in the public schools.*

Working Your Way Through This Book

At the end of each chapter in this book will be a question or two that is meant to allow you to interact with the ideas of the chapter in relation to students in your own classroom. You pick the students and how you might try to implement some of the ideas in the chapter in working with them. I would suggest that you get a journal (if you are into that type of thing) and record your answers so you can refer to them and have a plan to follow.

That suggests that you might best read through this book slowly. Any changes you wish to make in your teaching will come slowly anyway, and it is far better to ponder the ideas in the book, chew on what they mean in your particular situation, and then try to do something about them. That is what would make this become something more than just one more body of information to receive and one more book on your shelf. My goal is for it to make a difference in the way you teach and do things in your classroom, so after the ideas are presented, each chapter concludes with "Now What?" I hope you enjoy responding to the thoughts I present.

Part 1

Realities

1 Realities Our Students Face

Stories of Various Children

Children come to school from all kinds of backgrounds. The one thing they all have in common is that all are broken. Only the degree and manifestations of brokenness differ. The children are broken, and so are the families, churches, schools, and communities from which they come. So, they present big challenges to those of us who teach them.

Let's look at the lives of some children who cross the thresholds of our classrooms. These are all stories of real children in real classrooms reported to me by real teachers with names changed for obvious reasons. They come from a variety of schools, not all urban and poor. Almost all these children should be recognizable to teachers who work with children in public schools. I expect each teacher can remember someone who resembles a child or two in these scenarios.

Terrence. Terrence came to school in the first grade very intellectually behind. He lived with his grandmother in an impoverished urban neighborhood. Almost all his siblings and cousins were incarcerated by the time they were teenagers, and they would ridicule Terrence as he lay on the ground in a fetal position crying and yelling. When something went wrong at school, he would yell, cry, and dive under his desk.

Sonja. Sonja had been bounced from foster care home to foster care home over the past few years. She had entered the foster care system because of family abuse, and her brother had starved to death from neglect as a young child. She had a treatable life-threatening disease that involved the tissues in her body separating from one another. In her first week of school as a fourth grader, the retina detached from one of her eyes, and in the second week it happened in the other eye. She was then legally blind, and she had become very despondent. She was falling way behind in school.

LaToya. LaToya is in the eleventh grade and is one of six children in her family; all of the children have different fathers. Her mother is currently unemployed, and it is hard to know how and where the family gets food. LaToya has made references to being hungry. She has very few clothes. Her mother is currently dating a man who is mean to LaToya, and when he broke up with her mother, her mother tried to commit suicide. In school LaToya is very quiet and withdrawn.

Shawn. Shawn had gotten suspended for the entire year at his previous school, but when he came into a particular teacher's class, he had been very positive, upbeat, and diligent in his work. He said he was going to change his life, and it appeared that he was. One day he came to class late, and he was very quiet. When his fellow students were leaving, his head was on his desk and he was sobbing. The principal, a very tough disciplinarian, had seen Shawn in the hall and pulled him into his office to warn Shawn that he knew all about his past troubles and that he had better be careful because he was being watched all the time. The principal said he was not going to be trusted.

Sierra. Sierra is also a high school student who, by January of the school year, had been in four different schools, and she was doing very poorly in all of them. She currently had been ejected from her mother's house because she did not get along with her mother's boyfriend. Sierra was regularly thrown out of the house on a whim, and she tried to kill herself with too much alcohol, trying to numb the pain she felt. When she was a little girl, she was raped by her cousins. At school she was despondent and alone.

Joshua. Joshua is a sixth grader who was involved in asking classmates for food and sometimes taking it from them without asking. Upon investigation, it was determined that his single mom could not always provide food for the family. Joshua had watched his dad die in front of him a few years ago from heart issues. Joshua and his brothers had become involved in some gang activity in their neighborhood, and the family was forced to leave their home one night with only what they could carry. They rely on people in the neighborhood to get clothes, food, and furniture—for most of their basic needs. Joshua also has to keep his baby nephew at night while his older sister works to bring home some money for the family.

Darius. Darius is also a sixth grader who was hard to get to know, and he exhibited many behavior problems. His father was incarcerated—a fact that came out while reading a book in class that included a similar situation. The reason for one period of incarceration was sexual abuse in the home with one of Darius' siblings and a neighbor. Darius has four younger sisters, and he is definitely the man of the house in a government housing project, where there is no privacy at all. He lives in poverty, with a constant struggle for food, clothes, and bare necessities.

Maria. Maria comes from a home where the pressure to succeed is great. Her older siblings set a very high academic standard, and her parents expect her to live up to her siblings' performance. Her father is a doctor. He works long hours, and he is seldom home. Her mother was a beauty queen in college, and she also expects Maria to dress well, and generally to be perfect in appearance. Maria got caught cheating on her schoolwork, for the second time.

Leon. Leon is new to the school, and he has been to several different schools in his short time as a student. He has difficulty accepting responsibility for his actions. And he has a temper that sometimes flares out of control. One day he got into a scuffle with another boy, and he punched him as they lined up to leave the playground and return to school.

Lejou. Lejou came to school in the eighth grade. He had no knowledge of his father, and his mother was deployed with the navy. He had spent some of his childhood with his mom, but not all of it. Much was spent living with his sister and grandmother. When his sister married and moved out, Lejou became quite despondent. He did not interact with the other students; he wanted to just go off to read books by himself. As the other children in the class were working on a project that involved finding the meaning of their names, Lejou said his name did not mean anything, that his mom just made it up. Another part of the project involved telling stories about one's life. Lejou did not have any to tell, nor could his grandmother and sister provide any. He appeared to be almost a "zero."

Rick. Rick is a special education student in high school. All his previous teachers had generally given up on him, and he had been regularly suspended from the previous schools he had attended. He would never do the work his teachers asked of him, and he used profanity liberally. His mother is a drug addict, and his father was killed by "the other woman" in a love triangle. Rick had moved into a trailer with a friend, and then his mother moved in as well and began her drug dealing from there. He was going nowhere.

Ryan. Ryan's parents did not want Ryan, and they treated him very badly. The principal hated him. He was a bully, and he put another boy's head through a soda machine. A teacher described him as looking like a gangster out of the 1930s.

Robbie. Robbie is in the fourth grade. He has been held back for a year since he did not do well in the fourth grade in another school the previous year. He had missed a lot of school, and he was often bullied there. His mother has cerebral palsy, and his dad died when he was in second grade. Robbie is very independent; he gets himself wherever he needs to go, makes his own lunch, and does whatever he needs to do by himself. He also is a great skateboarder.

Charlie. Charlie is a four-year-old preschooler who lives with his grandmother because his parents are separated. He is high energy and very active, and he is a big child. Last year he was expelled from an after-school care program because he was punching people. He also has very little in the way of language skills, and he came to preschool not knowing much about colors, shapes, or numbers because he was not taught anything at home. His grandmother was afraid they would teach him "wrong."

Acacia. Acacia is in the sixth grade. Her parents died four years ago. She seems to be stuck emotionally and therefore also academically. She is moody, and she knows every button to push to get teachers mad. Rather than work in class, she will often draw and doodle and write notes with vulgar language in them. When disciplined, she gets angry and feels that the teacher is just out to get her.

Three Questions They All Ask

When Adam and Eve chose to disregard God's command to not eat of the tree of the knowledge of good and evil, they set into motion trouble that would plague every human being thereafter. Because they did not trust God, they were sent from the garden and their relationship with Him was broken. Before the fall, they knew who they were, and they were not ashamed of their nakedness (total vulnerability). They were secure in the love of God, who met with them, cared for them, and walked with them in the cool of the evening. They had no confusion about what they were to be doing as they worked freely in concert with God.

When they stopped believing and trusting God, they became afraid and ashamed. Cut off from God, they lost their way. Apart from God, it was hard to be sure of who they were, if they were safe, and what they were to be doing outside the garden. Since then every human being is born into a life in which these three questions consume our energies and attention: "Who am I?" "Will I be OK?" and "What am I to be about in life?"

Who am I? Before the fall, the identity of Adam and Eve was completely defined by their relationship to God. They were created in His image, they were of inestimable value (God declared them to be "very good"), they were loved, they were trusted with responsibility, and they were the object of God's delight. They did not have to wonder about who they were; it was as natural as their physical existence.

As we think about the students we have described who come into our classrooms, what can be said about their sense of identity? When you think of Sonja, does it appear that she has a great sense of identity? Does it seem that she has a sense of value?

Or let's take Maria. Do you suppose that she knows she is loved without condition? Or would her cheating suggest that she is desperately trying to find love somewhere or from someone and is having to do it through her performance?

Then there is Shawn. Do you think that he feels trusted? What would his reaction to the principal suggest?

Do you suppose that Sierra feels blessed and that she is the object of anyone's delight? Or does her despondence reveal that she has seldom if ever tasted of this?

What is Lejou telling us when he says his name does not mean anything when all the rest of the children in his class find their names in books and lists that describe some worthy characteristic?

Do you think Charlie thinks he is somebody though he has very few language skills and he does not know much of what the rest of the class knows?

Because we were created to be like God, to be in relationship with Him, to be valued, loved, trusted, and blessed, if we do not receive an identity including those things from God, we will create it in some other way. If we do not receive it from those who we deem to be important (parents, teachers, or other role models), we will likely seek it from anyone who shows the slightest likelihood of giving it to us, even if we have to do ugly, destructive, or harmful things to get it. Do you think that could be going on with your students who have difficulty in school and who disrupt your class and do not perform well on the things you give them to do?

Will I be OK? The question of security weighs in as heavily as the question of identity. Adam and Eve were completely safe in the garden, but outside they could not be sure of anything, and in fact they were told they would have trouble. It is no different for each of us. Much in the world is ugly and tough and unforgiving and uncertain. In the places we are supposed to be most assured we are safe (like home), we often are not safe at all.

Does this sound like part of the issue for Sonja? Do you think she feels safe at home? Anywhere? Why would she not feel safe?

Or let's take Joshua. How do you think he feels about knowing a gang is after him?

And then there is LaToya. Would she feel like she is really going to be OK though her mother has tried to kill herself and would leave LaToya and her five siblings?

Does it appear that Terrence feels safe when he dives under his desk when something goes wrong?

Why did Leon punch another boy over an issue on the playground?

Did it appear that Ryan feels OK about himself when he put another student's head through a soda machine?

How is Acacia going to feel secure and safe since both of her parents died when she was only in the second grade?

Again, we were created to be completely safe in our relationship with God. But that depends on trusting Him, something which Adam and Eve did not do. Being safe for our students involves their being able to trust the important people in their lives, something very hard to do when someone has been effectively orphaned, or betrayed, or shamed in life. But we have to get that feeling from someone, so if we don't get it from the right people, we will automatically seek it from the wrong people.

What am I to be about? God created us to have purpose, to jointly care for the creation with Him, to reveal His character to a watching world. But to do any of these things meaningfully, we again have to be in a relationship with Him. When that relationship is cut off because of sin, finding our purpose is a huge challenge.

We are supposed to get help from the important people in our lives. They are supposed to show us in an earthly way what the divine reality of the purpose of our lives is. But when the people in our lives hurt us, betray us, leave us hanging, ditch us, or use us, we are not likely to be encouraged in any purpose from them. And again, without it coming from the right places, it comes from the wrong places.

What would give Darius any sense of purpose in life? Or how about Sierra? What reason do they have for living? Why should they think there is something meaningful in life that should capture their hearts, imaginations, and energies?

Does it appear that Rick has any sense of what life could be for him?

Now What?

Describe two broken people (or groups of people) in your own current classroom experience who represent stories of brokenness. They don't have to represent the exact same problems described in this chapter; they just need to represent forms of brokenness that appear in the children who walk through your doors each day. Then, describe how you think they may lack the relationships, grace, and treatment as image bearers described in the introduction to this book.

2 Realities Teachers Face

Legal Constraints and Freedoms

In the first section of this chapter, you will find a description of the legal constraints and freedoms that Christian teachers have in public schools, as contributed by Finn Laursen, executive director of Christian Educators Association International (CEAI). He has graciously allowed me to include this story from his lengthy experience in public schools. He writes in the first person and tells a part of his own story even as he gives the guidelines for what teachers can and cannot do in regard to exercising their Christian faith in the public school classroom. Appendix B at the end of the book gives further information on CEAI and its services.

> **From Finn Laursen.** I have been blessed to be able to serve as a public school educator for thirty-two years. I was a middle school classroom teacher of English, a school counselor in middle school and high school, an assistant principal in middle school and high school, a high school principal, and a superintendent of schools. For the majority of that time, I was able to live out my Christian faith in those roles. Since 2003 I have served as executive director of Christian Educators Association International (CEAI), a professional association for Christian educators working in public and private schools.

Although I was churched all my life, I entered teaching without a personal relationship with the Lord. I experienced the personal transformation from "head knowledge" to "heart knowledge" while serving as a middle school counselor.

I had been trained in Rogerian counseling and had been taught never to direct the students we counsel. If there were not absolute truths, nondirective counseling makes sense. Once I made the commitment to be in relationship with the Lord and I was filled with His Spirit, the Bible came alive to me and I found absolute truths that could make an impact on how I counseled students.

For instance, I was counseling a seventh-grade boy I'll call Bobby. We all have known a Bobby; he had no interest in school or in achieving anything there, so there were no incentives teachers could use to control his behavior or motivate him to learn. Bobby was a continual disruption. He was regularly being sent to the office, where the ultimate punishment, suspension, could be administered. In Bobby's world, suspension was a desired outcome. Ultimately, he spent more time in the guidance office than at the principal's office or in class.

The Scripture that guided my time with Bobby was from Genesis: "God created man in His own image, in the image of God He created him" (1:27, NASB). I started treating Bobby as if he were created in God's image, and I started seeing him through God's eyes: a young man full of potential. I not only treated him as such but started verbalizing to him my high expectations for him. He never reached those expectations while in middle school, and he finally was expelled when he became violent with a teacher.

Years later as I was serving as a high school principal in another district, Bobby showed up in my doorway … I recognized him immediately. Bobby told me his story of quitting high school and becoming a drug dealer, overdosing near death, and doing time in prison. He told me about lying on his bunk in prison wanting to die and starting to remember some of the things I told him in middle school. That very day he invited Jesus into his life, and transformation started.

He said he had waited six months after his release from prison to look me up, wanting to make sure his conversion "stuck" outside of prison. He wanted me to know that my efforts with him had not been in vain. I then realized that those of us playing the role of missionaries in public school often plant the seeds that will be harvested later. Bobby had not realized that he had as much influence on my life as I had on his.

Once I understood that I was actually a full-time missionary placed in our public schools, my light started shining brightly and I did make a difference. That difference increased once I grasped the reality that I was not breaking any laws by being open about my faith.

As I was maturing as a Christian, I realized that understanding my legal freedoms was important so I could maneuver legally, but there were times when I should fall back on biblical principles rather than demanding my rights.

I remember receiving a note from a teacher, whom I'll call Betty, while I was serving as an assistant principal. Betty had asked me if I could meet with her during lunch and pray with her; I sent a message back to her telling her to meet me in my office. I usually did not take a break for lunch, but that day I made an exception. During our thirty minutes of prayer, I received no calls or knocks on my door—a clear sign of the Lord's presence since this never happened.

After school I was called to the principal's office and questioned about my activities with Betty. The principal had gone through my mailbox and found Betty's prayer request. The principal ordered me never to pray with a staff member again. My first reaction was to demand my right of constitutionally protected prayer: private prayer when off the clock.

Then the Holy Spirit brought to mind 1 Peter 2:18–20: "Servants, be submissive to your masters with all respect, not only to those who are good and gentle, but also to those who are unreasonable. For this *finds* favor, if for the sake of conscience toward God a person bears up under sorrows when suffering unjustly. For what credit is there if, when you sin and are harshly treated, you endure it with patience? But if when you do what is right and suffer for it you patiently endure it, this *finds* favor with God" (NASB).

In light of this truth, I explained to the principal that I had not sought out the teacher to pray, that this seemed like a "God appointment" during my off-the-clock time since we were not disturbed, but I would submit to his authority. I further described how I understood authority from the "heavenlies" down to the school building. I assured him that I would not seek teachers out to pray, but if such a "God appointment" would arise again and I submitted to his demand not to pray again, would he be accountable to God for my refusal to pray?

The room fell silent as he pondered my request … he actually turned pale and seemed uncomfortable. After a long silence he stood, pointed a finger at me and said, "OK, if you pray again, you *must* lock the door so people do not walk in and think we are some kind of cult here!" I agreed.

Six months later, the principal wandered into my office after school, shut my door, and said, "The next time you … you know … you talk to God … could you mention my wife? She has been diagnosed with breast cancer." Had I simply demanded my rights six months earlier, this request never would have been made.

I became firmly convinced that living out biblical principles on a daily basis was not only legal but should be a way of life for all Christians. The framers of this nation believed the same; from their roots of faith, they birthed a nation that was based on many of those truths. After all, most of the signers of the Declaration of Independence were committed Christians. Many of the signers believed in the Bible as the divine truth, and they believed in the God of Scripture and His personal intervention (Pelton 2008).

After they created the Declaration of Independence, the Continental Congress voted to purchase and import Bibles for the people of this country. As followers of Jesus, they understood the importance of building a nation on a firm foundation. That same congress birthed the American Bible Society to that same end.

Patrick Henry said, "It cannot be emphasized too strongly or too often that this great nation was founded not by religionists, but by Christians, not by religions, but by the gospel of Jesus Christ" (Mansfield 2001, 27). The concept of denying the Christian roots of this nation is a relatively new phenomenon, one I believe that has led many to deny their own faith and actually accept the lie that our public schools must be "God-free zones."

Our forefathers had great foresight when they penned the Constitution. They realized that building a strong nation could not happen without the help of the Lord, and in the First Amendment they made sure that the government would not establish a religion nor prohibit the expression of religion. At the Constitutional Convention, Benjamin Franklin, perhaps one of our most liberal forefathers, set the tone for the writing. He realized that they had been meeting to draft a guiding document for a new nation and had neglected seeking the Creator. After the following speech, overflowing with biblical allusions, all future sessions were commenced with prayer.

On June 28, 1787, Benjamin Franklin boldly said the following: "I have lived, Sir, a long time, and the longer I live, the more convincing proofs I see of this truth—that God Governs in the affairs of men. And if a sparrow cannot fall to the ground without His notice, is it probable that an empire can rise without His aid?" He continued: "We have been assured, Sir, in the Sacred Writings, that 'except the Lord build the House, they labor in vain that build it.' I firmly believe this, and I also believe that without His concurring aid we shall succeed in this political building no better than the Builders of Babel" (Federer 2000, 248–49).

James Madison, "the Father of the U.S. Constitution," said, "We have staked the whole future of American civilization, not upon the power of government, far from it. We have staked the future of all our political institutions upon the capacity of mankind for self-government; upon the capacity of each and all of us to govern ourselves, to control ourselves, to sustain ourselves according to the Ten Commandments of God" (Federer 2000, 411).

As our forefathers penned the Constitution, they ensured that future government agencies, like schools, would not control religion or silence the convictions of a religious people. The First Amendment of the United States Constitution states: "Congress shall make no law respecting an establishment of religion, or prohibiting the free exercise thereof …" This Establishment Clause declares that no government agency can act in any way to establish a religion or do anything to stop the expression of religion. Thus the government cannot force religious beliefs on others, and it cannot roadblock religious activity. The First Amendment also says that Congress can't make a law "abridging the freedom of speech, or of the press; or the right of the people peaceably to assemble, and to petition the Government for a redress of grievances." This Free Exercise Clause clarifies that the government cannot roadblock the freedom of speech that is so freely given to those living in this great nation.

How does the First Amendment make an impact on a public school teacher? Public school educators *can* do the following:

- Engage in personal prayer and Bible reading
- Attend student activities including prayer, Bible study, and worship
- Lead after-school religious activities for students such as Good News Club
- Share personal religious beliefs when asked or when appropriate within the curriculum
- Teach about religion or the Bible in curriculum
- Openly live according to their biblically based convictions
- Share faith issues with staff

Public school educators *cannot* do the following:

- Use their position to promote their religious convictions
- Inhibit student religious expression
- Teach the Bible to students devotionally during the school day
- Lead students in prayer in their role as educators
- Treat religious expression differently than nonreligious expression

The courts have equated teachers as arms of the government, since they are supported by public dollars. Thus a public school teacher cannot establish his or her religion in the classroom. In other words, Christian educators cannot use their public position to force their beliefs on students. However, the school staff cannot use its power to ban the free exercise of religion in the school.

I remember my first year as a high school principal. One of our teachers stopped in after school. I'll call him David. He was quite shaken by something that happened at the end of the day. David asked to meet behind closed doors, saying he had made a major error in judgment while left alone with a student. As I tried to settle him down in my office, my mind raced with the terrible acts he might have committed.

Then the truth surfaced; a student had stayed after class, shut the door after all other students had left, and asked this volatile question of his teacher: "Do you believe there is a god?" David's eyes bulged as he confessed, "Without thinking, I said, yes." He went on to explain that he realized now he had violated the separation of church and state by his bold confession. I had to assure him that there was nothing in any law or document requiring him to lie.

In my role of executive director of Christian Educators Association International (CEAI), I am continually confronted with such misunderstandings of the freedoms we have in this nation to speak openly about our faith. CEAI exists to help Christian educators understand and carry out their mission. CEAI provides resources such as magazines, newsletters, daily devotionals, and many other printed and digital resources from a biblical worldview (www.ceai.org).

Our public school students have total freedom of religious expression in school since they are not government employees. Students can lead prayer, read or distribute Bibles or other religious material, and openly discuss their faith publicly or through assignments. And they can be given the same access to facilities as others get for nonreligious activities. In other words, school employees must be "blind to religion." They cannot treat religious expression differently than nonreligious expression.

Precisely because there are so many negative influences bombarding public school students today, CEAI considers our public schools a mission field ripe for harvest. Through public schools we have access to many who will never enter our churches.

Like no other time in history, our children are bombarded nonstop with negative information. Media saturation has reached a level that our children who are starting in elementary school experience greater influence from outside the home than from within. They are exposed to a sexualization in our culture that has expanded to all areas and ages. Hard-core pornography is just a point and a click away, and many of our children are unintentionally being exposed to unimaginable perversions.

Few school-age children self-identify as Christian. Christian educators who interact daily with young people can have a life-changing effect on those who do not have a personal relationship with our Lord, and at the same time Christian educators can be powerful role models for Christian students on campus. (Finn Laursen, pers. comm.)

Logistical Constraints

At a gathering of Christian teachers who work in public schools, the seminar leader asked the teachers to describe some of the major challenges they experienced today in their classrooms. Here is a list of some of the things they mentioned:

- A lack of respect all around
- A lack of support from home
- More and more students coming from poverty and broken homes and backgrounds; students coming to school with a great deal of baggage and thus being very needy
- People being devalued in general
- School being a generally hostile environment—violence, bullying, little support even among peers
- Relativism in morality and students with very different values, lack of work ethic
- Student perceptions of reality
- Isolation in the faculty, as Christians feel very alone
- Too many roles the teacher is to play and not enough resources to meet the needs; not enough time to do what is required let alone what is needed
- State testing requirements controlling the curriculum, teaching, and evaluation of teachers
- Union pressure
- Being under a microscope for performance
- Temptation to fall into cynicism
- Blame placing

All these issues make teaching a great challenge. When you add the challenge of allowing your faith to be alive and influential in your classroom, you raise the bar of difficulty.

The Diversity in the Classroom

The diversity of abilities, motivations, backgrounds, and relationships of students in our classrooms is staggering. The first thing that comes to mind when we confront this reality is *difficulty*—a sense of being overwhelmed by trying to meet so many students in so many different places. Some may actually be interested in learning; some may be there only because they are not yet old enough to legally drop out. Some have high aspirations, and some have very low aspirations. Some are used to listening to authority, and others are only used to fighting with authority.

There are different faith backgrounds as well. Some are Christians, some may be Muslims, some are exposed only to superficial religion, and some are never exposed to anything religious at all. Some may want to talk about questions of faith, and others do not.

Then there is the matter of their relationships with other important people. Some may be relatively happy in their families, and others may feel emotional (and sometimes physical) torture at home. Some are very angry—at nearly everyone. Others may be very depressed about life. Some want to really be something in life; others may want to die. Some may find it fairly easy to trust us as teachers, and for others it seems that is not the least bit possible.

The classroom is certainly a microcosm of the world at large, with all its difficulties and challenges. More positively, the classroom is also a bucketful of possibilities. Dealing with such diversity provides us with more opportunity to be creative than we can mentally imagine. The unpredictability of it all leaves us in a great position to completely depend on God for anything positive to happen. If we don't think we have to fix everyone and solve every problem, and believe that is the Holy Spirit's job, we can exercise an extraordinary amount of freedom in responding to these children.

Whether we look at the difficulty or the opportunity (and in reality we ought to look at both), it is important to believe (and act upon the belief) that we can adhere to a manageable number of convictions about ourselves, our students, the process of learning, and the whole educational endeavor and learn to apply those principles in diverse ways to meet our diverse students where they live. That is what it will mean for us to be "incarnational" as disciples of Jesus ourselves. It will also allow us to invite our students to become disciples as well.

Asking the Same Three Questions as the Students

All these constraints and issues come from external sources. But there are also internal constraints and issues. Teachers are as diverse as students, and we ask the same big three questions our students ask: "Who am I?" "Will I be OK?" and "What am I to be about?" Because we are born into the same fallen situation as our students, sometimes our attempts at answers are as distorted as those of the students. We have just learned to distort in more socially acceptable ways. Even as those who have a restored relationship with God, we still are affected by sin and its distortions.

None of us grew up in a perfect environment or with a perfect relationship with a heavenly Father. We were all shaped by our experiences with parents, teachers, pastors, friends, and other significant people. And the process of our renewal is sometimes long and even painful.

Even those of us who grew up in basically healthy homes do not escape. Our own fallen nature takes us to find our identity, security, and purpose in something other than God. A fallen self is a self that is desperate to put itself back on track. We have the sense that *we* must do it ourselves. And the culture around us says "Of course you do!"

Then we also have an enemy who constantly whispers to us the same lie he hissed to Eve—"Surely God did not mean what He said; trust yourself, not Him. What He says is all way too good to be true; you have to do *something* to be somebody and be OK." The forces against us are powerful, and we must not take them lightly just because we are basically functional and socially adept.

The way we answer the big three questions will greatly affect how we view, and interact with, our students. Thus, we need to discover, and surrender, some of our own distorted answers to the questions. The most common wrong answers we have are those that suggest we find our identity, security, and purpose through what we have, what we can do, and what we achieve. Or, we could say through possession, power, and success.

Most teachers do not have enough material possessions to find much identity, security, or purpose in them. That is not the kind of possession that would trip us up. Our possessions would be things like personality and intellect; maybe some of us would have good looks or other personal skills and abilities that might make us desirable. If students like me, I could find an identity in that, especially if I am recognized for my contribution to student life. If I am judged to be really sharp in my field and get along well with others, I could find some sense of identity there too. If I am respected by my peers, I can believe I have some value.

If I have been successful as a student myself, or as a teacher, or as anything else, I think I can find some security in that—especially if I am judged as superior to others. Success in almost anything can be used to give me a sense of being OK; after all, I have accomplished something. And how many of us can admit that we think of ourselves primarily in terms of what we do (giving us our identity), and then the degree to which we are successful at it gives us our sense of security?

When we consider what we are to be about, we have a few ways we can try to answer that question. The first would be in terms of what we think we want to do in order to *be* somebody. That which might give us some sense of identity and security could direct our search for purpose. Another way we try to answer that question is to get some trusted person or people to tell us what we should be about. Or sometimes a powerful person we need to please will try to impose it on us. That may be a parent, a spouse, or any person who is important to us. A third, more "spiritual" way is to ask God to tell us. We are willing to be about whatever He wants us to, as long as He will just tell us what it is. We are willing servants; we just need some orders.

While these answers from the world, the devil, and our flesh (the unholy trinity) may be much more socially acceptable than the ones our students pursue, they are no less destructive, fruitless, and dishonoring to God. They all reveal the continuing brokenness in the relationship between God and us. They all still tend to exhibit distrust in God, they deny who we now are in Christ, they rob God of His glory, and they leave us weary, fearful, and unfulfilled. We definitely need something better, just as our students do.

Now What?

Describe the realities you face that make it difficult for you to personally have a healthy relationship with the students you identified at the end of chapter 1. Also, what hinders your ability to treat them with grace? and as image bearers?

3 Broken Realities and Grace

When we consider how God chose to deal with the broken reality of a world and a people beset by sin, it is imperative that we realize His means was *grace*. He chose to do so because that was the nature of His character. It was not an easy or painless choice; rather it was extremely costly for Him. However, it was the only way to reach His lost and broken children. Law only pushed them further away and condemned them.

As God's chosen representatives and image bearers, we are called to deal with broken people in a broken world in the same manner. Over the course of the years a student spends in school, we have an extraordinary opportunity to be the conduits of God's grace to the very broken, diverse students who come to our classrooms day after day, year after year. *We have the incredible privilege of demonstrating to our students just who God is by the way we do things in our classrooms.*

For this to happen, our classrooms must operate in an ethos of grace. Grace must pervade all our interactions with students and all we do in the classroom. We are to be a living definition of grace and to offer it to those whom God sends our way as students.

This is not typical as schools tend to operate very much in an ethos of law— students do this and they get that. Students get exactly what they deserve—no more, no less. They are good, and they are given favor. They are bad, and they are given punishment. I once was told (very adamantly!) by a Christian teacher that God may operate by grace, but schools operate by law! Yes, they often do, but in that process they do not show forth the face or heart of God and thus teach their students to live by something other than the gospel.

If these things are true, it would be fairly important to spend a bit of time considering just what grace is, and what it is not, before we try to apply it to our work as teachers.

Just What Is This Thing Called Grace?

Grace is recognized as God's undeserved favor to sinners (Douglas 1962). As fallen sinners we could not have lived righteously enough to satisfy God's holy demands (Romans 3:10–12). Thus we had no hope of ever being reconciled to Him. We were under condemnation and were, in fact, already spiritually dead (Ephesians 2:1). Restoring us to life was God's act of pure grace (Romans 3:24, Ephesians 2:8–9). What we could not perform, God performed for us in Christ. Jesus kept the law that we could not keep, and we became the beneficiaries of His perfect performance. God imputed to humankind, who did not deserve it, the very righteousness of Christ that satisfied Him.

While the mercy of God keeps us from getting what we deserve, the grace of God gives us the *opposite* of what we deserve—His favor instead of His condemnation. Instead of death, we receive life. Instead of a "guilty" sentence, we receive a declaration of righteousness. Instead of living with the penalty of the curse, we have been created anew to live as image bearers, reflecting God in our thoughts and actions. On this side of heaven, the reflection is not perfect, but through the Spirit it *still* shows the world that God is the truth.

Christians know that it is by grace through faith in Christ that we are saved and justified. Most of us would also agree that we are glorified (when we depart from this life to be with Christ) by grace, but it is often a different story when it comes to living day by day through grace. That is a concept that is harder to receive. It is much more common to live by a legalistic "do this and you get that" mentality, the same mentality that is so prevalent in our schools.

Grace does not entail receiving our just reward. It involves receiving something that we have done absolutely nothing to earn, receiving a blessing when our just reward is punishment and being loved when we deserve judgment. Our work deserves an F, and we are given someone else's A. To top it off, the one who gives us the A is delighted to do so, and so is the one who "earned" the A in the first place! This grace is the very heart of the gospel that we encourage our students to follow in their daily lives. Sounds outrageous, doesn't it? The grace of God is *indeed* outrageous! In fact, it is so outrageous that we are unable to appropriate it in the way our institutions and organizations function or even in the way we relate to one another.

The *process* content of "do this and you get that" teaches that the rewards we receive are just what we earn—we get what we deserve. What we deserve is determined by someone else's judgment of how we perform in comparison with that person's expectations. If we do not receive good rewards, we do not deserve them because we have not done well enough—from the evaluator's perspective. If we do not deserve a reward, we may feel that there is something wrong with us and we are not as worthy as those who do receive rewards. The obvious remedy is to do better, or to quit or try to smash the system. We can always change our ideas about whose judgment is important to us. If we cannot get the grades our teachers or parents want us to get, we may be able to get the attention and admiration of our peers by acting up in class with them or by breaking rules with them. Somehow we will surely be able to live up to someone's expectations and thus be accepted and valued.

The obvious problem with this method is that it doesn't work. It never really satisfies or fulfills because it does not deal with the real problem—namely, the broken, fallen, sinful, empty heart of the person who needs to be loved and accepted. Because of a fallen nature, this person can never adequately live up to expectations. Therefore, such a person continues to live in the shame, false appearances, denial, and fear that characterized Adam and Eve. There is no hope, grace, or life in this behavior. Even keeping the law most of the time is not enough, for God tells us that failure in even one point is sufficient to bring condemnation and death.

If the verbal content that we teach our students could overcome the process content, the problem would not be hard to solve. But the process content is what sticks most readily and deeply with the student. Students generally receive the verbal content passively as if we poured it into their heads. They memorize it and learn the information, with a minimum of personal involvement. The process content is the one they experience, and the learning is more active as they actually live it. This learning involves more than cerebral activity. It involves their emotions and sense of well-being—their whole self! No wonder it sticks longer, and no wonder it is the learning that directs their lives after school is over.

Consequently, if our students are to be affected by the grace of the gospel, they must experience it in their learning environment. In cases of broken and very hurtful home environments, there is little likelihood they will experience it there. In relation to equally troubled peers, it is not likely they will experience it there. The culture certainly will not demonstrate it to them. We as teachers may be one of the very few sources through whom they could experience it.

We must examine our personal relationships with the students, attitudes toward the students, classroom management practices, grading and measurement practices, the structure of our curriculum and daily learning activities—every part of our learning atmosphere—to see whether our students are breathing the fresh air of the gospel that leads to life or the toxic fumes of legalism that lead to death.

Accepting It for Ourselves

The apostle Paul told the Philippians that he was confident "that he who began a good work in you will carry it on to completion until the day of Christ Jesus" (Philippians 1:6). He, being Christ, is the one who is doing the work through His grace. John Newton understood this as well. His famous hymn "Amazing Grace" speaks of grace teaching his heart to fear, relieving that fear (salvation), carrying him safely, and finally leading him home (seemingly a reference to his sanctification and glorification). Paul addresses the Romans in similar fashion: "Therefore, since we have been justified through faith, we have peace with God through our Lord Jesus Christ, through whom we have gained access by faith into this grace in which we now stand. And we rejoice in the hope of the glory of God" (Romans 5:1–2). We were saved by grace, we live by grace, and we will be taken to heaven by grace.

We exist only by God's grace from one day to the next, for each time we fail at even one point of the law, we deserve condemnation (Galatians 3:10). Who, by virtue of motive or action, does not fail at many points each day? By faith, believing God has forgiven us through the blood of His Son, we now stand approved before God in the righteousness of Christ. His righteousness gives us continued favor with God. Through the Spirit, we now desire righteousness, and we are enabled to act righteously even though our righteousness could never be enough to satisfy God.

Therefore, grace enables us not only to be redeemed but to act redemptively. We cannot live, or teach, redemptively except by an awareness and an experience of God's grace that motivates us. We cannot live, or teach, redemptively unless we are daily demonstrating what His grace is all about. If we have experienced redemption through grace, we will live out that redemption through grace. As reconciliation and restoration of our relationship with God came through grace, so will our image-bearing activities of renewal.

Grace in Our Schools: Some Beginning Thoughts

What, then, does this all mean to us as Christian teachers in the classroom? To start with, when the world watches us teach redemptively, they should not see a people who are finally "getting it right." Rather, they should see a band of sinners, broken and fallen but healed, who now live freely and explore eagerly in the hope, grace, forgiveness, and righteousness of Christ (Ephesians 2:4–7). We are recipients of grace, and we must live in gratitude for that grace without thinking more highly of ourselves than we ought.

Likewise, we are free from bondage to sin and released from the curse of the law. The law is a schoolmaster, a babysitter if you will, to protect us, to keep us from harm, to remind us of what we should do. In that role, and because the law came from God, it is good. But the law also imprisons us apart from faith (Galatians 3:23), though its purpose is to lead us to Christ—to show us how utterly incapable of keeping the law we are and how totally dependent upon His grace we are. When we think that keeping the law will somehow add to, or make possible, our sanctification, or that reasonably keeping the law will somehow assure us of God's favor, we completely miss the meaning and reality of the gospel.

Therefore, our classrooms and schools must be places where law is not the reigning king, but rather where the grace-full Christ is King. We demonstrate that trait when, as recipients of grace, we become dispensers of it as well. In particular, we should no longer operate under the curse with students and teachers trying to control each other to get what they want. The watching world should no longer see us creating an atmosphere where performance is the name of the game—do what we ask and you will get your just reward, don't do it and you will get your just punishment. If God has performed the legal act of blotting out our transgressions and the relational act of "remembering them no more" (Bridges 1991), then systematic punishment for wrongdoing or failure is not the response of grace, and neither is the systematic giving of a blessing for sufficient obedience.

Consequences for behavior are rightful and necessary to help children become what God created them to be, and God clearly disciplines the children He loves (Hebrews 12:6). But a proper inclusion of consequences is far more than rewards for achievement and punishment for failure. If God has hurled our sins into the sea (Micah 7:19), removed our transgressions from us as far as the east is from the west (Psalm 103:12), and put all our sins behind His back (Isaiah 38:17); and if He gives His grace to a broken, inconsistent, and unfaithful servant like Samson and offers forgiveness to a thief on a cross who can do nothing to earn any points, surely we must do the same when we deal with our students' sins and failures in school. If God looks at us and sees the righteousness of Christ, surely we must look at our students and see something besides their good or bad deeds, their high or low achievement.

Redemption is an act of grace. It is given to us because of God's grace, and we even receive it through grace, for in our fallen state we would not be prone to receive it at all. In fact, our flesh still resists grace. In our flesh, we are determined to produce something in us that will give God reason to accept and love us. If redemption is rooted in grace, then redemptive teaching must likewise be rooted. Redemptive teaching is done in an atmosphere of grace where students and teachers alike can breathe blessing and life instead of the curse and death. Redemptive teaching is an act of grace, it is done because of grace, it occurs through grace, and it is a living demonstration of grace.

Classrooms and schools with grace as the prevailing atmosphere do not look at the issue of motivation in the same way as most schools. When grace is truly experienced, the response is gratitude and love—a motivation quite different from competition, reward, and avoidance of punishment. *Motivation that is a response to being loved is quite different from motivation that is a response to being threatened.*

The learning process is viewed differently as well, with the experience of grace occurring as much during the process of exploration as in the results of it. Even being allowed to explore instead of simply absorbing what one is told is a testimony to grace. For without grace, what teacher would have the nerve to let students explore and ask questions and create ideas? Success and failure in learning produce more than just a reward or punishment for the degree of accomplishment. Grace allows us to appreciate and embrace the unsolved mysteries of our inquiry as well as the identified problems we are able to "solve." Instead of being consumed with finding the answers so we can exercise control over things (or worse yet, just to prove that we have the answers), we might learn to appreciate the sovereignty of God precisely because we cannot know enough to find the answers and thus gain control.

Curriculum is not necessarily designed in the prevailing ways either. Curriculum choices that are designed to help students experience grace are not necessarily determined simply by what is in the textbooks or what is in the state curriculum guidelines. (Such guidelines cannot be set aside, but perhaps they do not need to rule as completely as we tend to let them.) A curriculum should expect more than a mastery of certain bodies of information. It should force students into situations in which they are challenged to both receive and give grace to others and in which their knowledge is not measured simply by written activity. Perhaps it will also lead one to an experience of awe and wonder that is deemed as valuable as achievement test scores.

Classroom management and discipline in a redemptive teacher's classroom is not based simply on a system of threats or rewards and punishments, which tend to treat students more like dogs than human beings. Instead of merely trying to control behavior and feelings, the focus is on affirming value and identity as image bearers of God—whether the student cares about God or not. The atmosphere provides students with the freedom and challenge of making choices and being responsible for them rather than forcing the students to comply with rules only for the sake of order.

And of course we need to recognize that as God has given us grace, He was humbled as He walked in our mess with us. So as teachers, we must be willing to be humbled and walk in the mess that students create as we attempt to show grace and change their lives. Classrooms with grace as the prevailing atmosphere are not necessarily characterized by outward order and spectacular test results, but they might be full of students who are tasting, and being affected by, the love of Jesus.

Measurement, evaluation, and grading probably do not look quite the same either. Everything is not so cut and dried, dependent simply on quiz and test performance, or determined solely by the teacher. God in His grace is not so interested in "paying" us (by our grades) in terms of what we deserve by our performance (see the parable of the workers in the vineyard). Rather, He seems to involve us in the process of much self-evaluation, give repeated opportunities for us to get up and try again, and continue to actually pick us up and reassure us so we can try again. Through all these acts He demonstrates generosity—quite a challenge for a teacher to emulate.

Perspectives to Help Build an Ethos of Grace

Following are some perspectives from an alternative high school operated from the framework of Christian principles and biblical beliefs. The students who attend this school have all struggled in school in some way or have been in the kind of trouble that has kept them from succeeding in any normal school setting. This is a school where grace is in place, and it has the same impact that the grace of Jesus had on His broken followers. Here are some of the perspectives that help create the atmosphere of the school:

- The behavior of students is ultimately determined by their own choices, and it is their personal responsibility.
- Our school has only three rules. Otherwise, questions, dilemmas, and arguments are worked through in a kind, respectful, gentle, and nonlecturing way.
- For both students and teachers, forgiveness is one of the main ways to deal with offenders. Forgiveness is not withheld until it is earned by good behavior or until the students have paid a sufficient price. Love is not withheld until students deserve it. Trust is not kept back until students prove they can be trusted.
- At our school, we often help students narrow their behavior choices to only a few options, all of which are acceptable to us and all of which are presented without lecturing. We lead and teach, but we do not coerce, entice, or threaten.
- No discipline is viewed as merely an end in itself. It always seeks to restore, since that is what redemptive disciplining should do.
- God means for us to learn from consequences, but it does not follow that He delivers consequences in order to ensure that we will behave in a certain way in the future.
- It is not our job to somehow eradicate sin or make students behave rightly.

- We rely on the movement of the Spirit of God in the students and the teachers rather than on management systems. We do not need to control as much as we need to shepherd.
- The spirit to empower good behavior comes through the way in which we grant that power to students, by not focusing on what is wrong in them but instead attempting to tap into what is good in them—the image of God and, for the believers among them, the spirit of Christ who now lives in them. If we treat them as image bearers, we invite them, and expect them, to live as such—just as God does.

You can probably see that approaching students in this manner creates quite a challenge for a teacher. You must not think that this approach means life will flow smoothly. Quite the contrary, it is very messy. Students sometimes still drop out, and some are suspended for a time. There is no lack of discipline; you can see that it is just handled in a very different way. Later in the book we will look more specifically at what grace means in the classroom in various arenas besides just discipline. But we must address one last concern before we move on—the common misunderstandings of grace.

Misunderstandings of Grace

Though grace is probably the most crucial doctrine in the Bible for helping us live as God desires, it is undoubtedly one of the most misunderstood, mistrusted, and misused doctrines of the Christian life. As mentioned earlier, we do not receive grace readily. It takes everything away from us and puts it all in God's hands. It makes Him look too good to be true and us too bad to be acceptable. We can earn nothing, and He gives us everything. When we deserve the penalty of death, He gives us the blessing of eternal life. Such cannot readily be comprehended by finite, sinful minds. Since it is not easily comprehended, grace also is often not easily received. Consequently, we do all sorts of wrong things with the amazing reality of grace.

Some people think that if grace is true, justice and discipline must then be eliminated. Justice and mercy cannot seem to coexist. This is not so, however. Justice was accomplished at the Cross. God did not overlook our sin; He emptied His full wrath toward it on Jesus. The price was paid, but by God, not us. At the Cross, justice and mercy kissed. At times, should teachers extend mercy and pay the price for students' failures? Can a teacher exhibit justice and mercy simultaneously, or is that ability something that we cannot emulate but only talk about since only God has the power to do it?

An experience of God's justice works its way into our understanding of discipline also through another means. Part of God's creational design is that acts do have consequences. In the world of nature those consequences are, well, "natural." We push a rock off a cliff, and it falls. In the world of relationships and culture building, people often deliver the consequences to others. "If a man will not work, he shall not eat" (2 Thessalonians 3:10). To follow God's created design, such consequences should be as "natural" as possible, and logically related to the behavior—good or bad. But the consequences can never be thought of as used by God to *ensure* right behavior in the future. God is not the great behavior modification expert in the sky.

To discipline is to create an environment in which students can make wise choices from within, not simply be rewarded or punished from the outside (VanVonderen 1992). Consequences are a significant, though not necessarily dominant, part of that environment. They help students make choices. God disciplines those He loves by telling us the consequences of certain behavior and allowing us to choose our actions. Then He lets the natural consequences follow, unless He sometimes chooses to break in and stop them. How, when, and why He chooses to sometimes intercede to protect us from the natural consequences of our actions is a mystery to us; it is supernatural, but it does happen.

Teachers should also discipline by identifying consequences of different behaviors and letting students choose which behavior they will pursue. The promised consequences must follow. But teachers are also given the authority to intervene and not deliver the expected consequences, as they are led by the Spirit. This is an important part of our discipline, since to rely solely on the consistent delivery of consequences often leads to discipline by a "system" rather than a person. God's discipline is always personal, and it is never simply through a system. His discipline is aimed at building a godly character on the inside through understanding our value in Christ, not just developing outward conformity to rules and expectations. It is a matter of choice, not control.

Another misunderstanding of grace is that it will simply free our sinful nature to come out and deny our responsibility to be obedient. However, those who turn grace into a license to sin have not had a true experience of grace. Only a counterfeit understanding of grace could lead one to that outcome.

There is no denial that grace leads to freedom—that was its intent. We were created to respond freely to God, and redemption once again gives us the power to respond in conjunction with His will instead of always against it. Since we still live in the flesh and in a fallen world, the use of that freedom does not always result in what it should. That fact, however, did not deter God in the first place, nor does it deter Him in dealing with us now. As indicated above, redeeming us was messy and ugly for God. We do not always use our freedom appropriately. Living with us in not-yet-glorified bodies is still messy for Him. Should we think that dealing with fallen students will be, or should be, any different? Do we think that somehow landing on the right outer structure, the right way of doing things, or the right set of rules and consequences will somehow correct the "inside" problem and make everything run smoothly?

Why do we think the supreme end is to have things run smoothly anyway? Probably because we use outward performance as a standard against which we measure our own standing and value before God (and other human beings), and if the students behave and learn as they should, we can take responsibility for what happened and feel good about ourselves as God's servants. If they do not do well, we take responsibility for that as well and feel there must be something wrong with us. In so doing, we fail to take responsibility for *our* job—creating an environment where they can make the right choices from the heart—and instead take on their responsibility—actually *making* those right choices.

Finally, obedience is the result of receiving God's grace, not the precursor to it. We do not receive God's grace because we have done the right things or because we had the right motives and desires. We do not receive it because we have sought to be obedient. If any of these reasons were the case, we could not call it grace because we would have done something to earn or deserve it. Rather, obedience follows from our love for God. Jesus said, "If you love me, you will obey what I command" (John 14:15). In many places, we see loving God and obeying His commands as tied inextricably together. If we understand our fallen nature and the grace of God correctly, however, we cannot subtly turn this into a works arrangement.

Obedience seems to be "proof" of sorts that we do indeed love Jesus. That is because if we truly love Him, the only thing that can follow will be obedience to His command (which, by the way, we see later is the command that we are to love one another as He has loved us). Obedience flows from our love. It does not somehow generate or increase our love. Since our love is a result of His having graciously loved us first, it appears that our obedience would be a result of our having been embraced by His love and immersed in His grace. (Those who do not obey do not lack experience with the law as much as they lack experience with the gospel.) Obedience that comes about in any other way is a work that is meant to gain us some favor with God. Such a work destroys the gospel and makes Jesus of no value to us (Galatians 5:2).

Thus we can hardly see grace as a force that denies our responsibility to be obedient. On the contrary, it is the only acceptable motive and means through which obedience can be pleasing to God. True grace brings true obedience, and obedience is a testimony to the presence of grace. Outward conformity to rules and expectations can fool us, so we must be careful of accepting such outward appearances. Obedience that emanates from a desire to earn God's favor, cement our status with Him, or impress others (and ourselves) with our spirituality is a grave offense to God, as it makes grace unnecessary.

Now What?

Imagine, and then describe, what it might look like if grace were the prevailing atmosphere in your interactions with the students you identified at the end of chapter 1.

Part 2

Understanding Ourselves

4 Teachers as Image Bearers

The Scriptures provide evidence that God holds teachers in high regard. Teachers are both gifted by God and held responsible to Him (James 3:1). In the church He gives some people the gift to teach (1 Corinthians 12:28, Ephesians 4:11), and in families He exhorts fathers to teach their children (Deuteronomy 4:9, 11:19). Perhaps the most significant evidence of God's concern for teachers is that He sent His very own Son not only to save His chosen people but also to teach them.

Teachers must also recognize themselves as human beings, created in the image of God, yet fallen, and through faith in Christ redeemed and restored. Consider several beliefs about the nature of human beings that are relevant for our discussion of who we are as teachers.

Active, Purposeful, and in Control

Teachers are called to be in charge of what is happening in the classroom. Help may be available from teacher manuals, curriculum guides, state mandates, or achievement test demands, but none of these can be the controlling factor in the way a teacher approaches teaching and learning. Sadly, many publishers (secular and Christian alike) deem it their duty to prescribe exactly what should be done each moment in the classroom. They provide the objectives, determine the content, outline the activities, write the discussion and test questions, and sometimes even determine the rewards for good performance.

Such an approach requires little of teachers other than a mechanical performance of what someone else (who has no knowledge of the local children and classroom) has deemed is right. Some publishers view teachers as possible stumbling blocks to learning and make all decisions for them. Others realize that teachers typically demand all the tools and suggestions the publisher can provide or they will view the materials with disfavor. Some school boards insist that teachers follow to the letter the curriculum guides and daily activities prescribed by the publishers, assuming this practice will ensure quality education. All these perspectives tend to undermine any worthwhile effort by the teacher to control the classroom. The teacher is reduced to a robot performing the tasks programmed into the process.

Contrary to the practices encouraged by such authors and publishers, it is up to the teachers to direct the learning process by weaving a meaningful tapestry of learning activities from what they know about the students, the information that should be acquired and used, the goals of learning appropriate to the students and their community, and the needs of society in the current and historical context. To do so, teachers must be in charge, not the curriculum guide. Textbooks are resources, not dictators of what will be learned. To give up the responsibility of determining how the texts will be used, what items of study will be emphasized, and what questions should be asked is to give up part of what it means for a teacher to bear the image of God.

A Creative, Thinking Being

As God gave human beings the responsibility to exercise control over the world around them and to develop its potential, He called them to do it creatively and rationally. Thus teachers are not simply to be in charge as noted above; they are to be *creatively* in charge. The importance of creativity is underscored by the fact that God's first recorded act in Scripture is creating. As we look at the way God has controlled the unfolding of history and acted on behalf of His people, we see a very creative mind at work, not one that is stymied by circumstances, short on imagination, mechanical, or determined by someone else.

Think for a moment about the amazingly creative ways in which He provided salvation for His people (Isaiah 9:6–7, Romans 5:6–8), left us a written revelation of Himself (2 Timothy 3:16, 2 Peter 1:21), led His people out of Egypt (Exodus 2–18), preserved His people throughout history (Genesis 45:5–7, Ezra 9:6–8, Jeremiah 29:1–14), and spread the message of His gospel. God has exercised control in creative ways, and teachers are called to do the same, *not* to be slaves to a curriculum guide or a teacher manual.

But just as God did not act creatively according to a whim, neither should teachers. They must use rational, carefully developed, and researched thought in bringing everything known about learning into the learning process. Teachers must take what is true and important about learning in general and creatively combine that knowledge with what they know about the immediate teaching and learning situation. Creative thinking is not an accident; it takes hard work and diligent effort. Teachers who simply follow the manual may often be taking the easy way out and succumbing to the pressures of time and the dictates of others who demand that a certain amount of material be covered.

Let me hasten to add that in spite of what I am saying, I do not think teacher manuals or curriculum guides need to be eliminated. On the contrary, we need carefully planned guidance. My complaint is about the way teachers use them and the way some publishers and administrators expect them to be used. Instead of being tools in teachers' hands, they tend to dictate the classroom experience and deny teachers the opportunity to fulfill a weighty part of the calling to live out the image of God. Any teacher who is serious about the thinking, creative dimensions of God's character should strenuously object to being controlled by curriculum guides and teacher manuals.

While teachers often complain that their students seem to do very little thinking, teachers who simply follow the manual should understand that they are actually contributing to the problem. Students seldom learn to think under the tutelage of teachers who do not think either. Nonthinking teachers are simply part of a cultural "how do I do it?" mentality. The world clamors for manuals on how to do everything from fixing cars to fixing broken marriages to fixing relationships with God. There seems to be no differentiation between manuals designed for what is truly mechanical and what is intensely personal—the latter demanding both creativity and rational thought. If we as teachers cannot creatively design experiences that will foster personal, meaningful learning, there is little hope that our students will rise above the mechanical in their approach to life.

Free and Responsible

Obviously, one must be free to make choices and be responsible for those choices in order to carry out the previous ideas. And of course God made us that way (Genesis 2:15–16, 3:6; Deuteronomy 30:11–20; John 7:17). Freedom and responsibility are necessary parameters for a creative, thinking manager.

A proper understanding of this freedom is important, however. First of all, it means we are free to use teacher manuals and curriculum guides as we carefully design our classroom work. Or we are free to modify them or not to use them. It also means that we may create our own guides and then modify or reject them later. But our freedom to use others' guides or create our own exists only as long as we are willing to use them within biblical guidelines for the educational process.

For instance, if a curriculum guide calls for activities that tend to treat our students as something less than beings made in the image of God, we are responsible for modifying the activities. Some curriculum guides and teacher manuals provide all the test questions for a given unit of study, and not a single question requires the student to think, only to recall items and events. These guides follow the same pattern throughout the course of study. They violate a fundamental biblical principle by not treating the learner as a thinking being, and therefore we are not free to use these guides as they stand.

Second, we are free to experience God's presence and pleasure in what we are doing (Psalm 16:7–11). As teachers, we need not be strangled by unrealistic expectations: that we will cover all chapters in the book, that our students will perform exceptionally on standardized tests, that our school will rank higher in achievement than other schools, or that our school will prepare students for the best prep schools or universities. We work hard and do as well as we can in our creative endeavors, but not to prove anything to ourselves or others or to achieve personal success and recognition. We strive for excellence because we love God and because we wish to give our work as an offering to Him—as unblemished as we can make it.

But we also understand that we are coworkers with Him, not working alone in trying to please Him. He is present with us, and we are to experience the pleasure of His presence in our work now as well as in eternity. Too often, as we are bound by the expectations and demands of immediate educational goals, we may lose sight of the fact that He participates in the work with us. He desires that we be free enough from external demands to focus on the joy of His presence as much in doing the work as in seeing the outcome. The outcome is not under our control anyway; it is under God's control. How unfortunate it is for us to miss the joy of His pleasure while actually doing His work because we are so driven toward the ends we have in sight. Putting it in strictly human terms, how much more complete and fulfilling it is to work toward a common goal side by side with someone you love than to work alone, hoping that the one you love will finally approve of what you have done by yourself!

Finally, we should understand that just as we are free to explore and be creative in our God-given role as teachers, we are also free to fail. Failure has such negative connotations in our culture, and yet God uses it in such positive ways. Failure is not our goal, but we should willingly accept it as part of the process of growing and serving God. We need not fear it, but rather we need to learn to capitalize on it and stop punishing ourselves and our students for it. The freedom to do that can only come from realizing that we rest securely in God's arms and that He is a sovereign God. The outcome is in His hands, but so is the process! Because God by His choice and work has saved us and is also sanctifying us, we are safe! Consequently, when failure and mistakes occur, we can creatively and fearlessly build them into the learning process.

We do not always need to simply punish our students with bad grades or ourselves with guilt feelings. We can learn to feel God's presence even in our failure. We might even learn not to take ourselves too seriously. What freedom that would be!

I suspect that the responsibility accompanying this freedom involves not only the obvious—accepting the consequences of our choices whether they lead to success or failure—but also the realization that we indeed must continually respond creatively to whatever happens as a result of our free choices. We choose, act, and deal with the results by making another choice, acting, and then dealing with more results. To accept this as part of our existence and to experience God's presence in it is to know something of what it means to walk with God. It is part of what it means to know the joy of the Lord in the midst of any set of circumstances. We choose and act again precisely because we know God is involved. Being responsible means we keep on going because God does.

We may often have a more fatalistic attitude toward the results of our actions and choices, sometimes even finding someone or something else to blame. While elements beyond a teacher's control frequently have an impact on success or failure in the classroom, blaming those elements may cause the teacher to give up the responsibility to be creative, thoughtful, or persistent in dealing with the situation. That is one reason why the success or failure of a particular teaching technique must not be the only determiner of whether we will use the technique again. If being responsible before God means we keep on responding, success or failure is simply one source of input used in creatively trying to determine what to do next.

Finite and Fallen

We must accept both the limitations and the possibilities that result from our own finite, fallen, and redeemed state. We are not God, but we are called to think His thoughts and to act like Him, sharing in His work and experiencing the joy of doing it with Him. The fall wreaked havoc with that purpose, but God was not thwarted. Instead, He triumphed.

The limitations placed on us by our finiteness are many, and they should point us to our reliance on the one who created us. Teachers cannot know for certain all there is to know about the learner, the learning process, the particular elements in the immediate situation, or the history that has affected the learner. We must have sufficient communication with the Father so that the Spirit will move us to right understandings and right choices. We must also be willing to recognize the place of the Holy Spirit in moving and shaping the thinking and lives of our students.

Recognizing it is not enough, though; we must pray for it diligently. Prayer for and with students is a significant response to the limitations of our finite nature.

The distortions that flow from our fallen state should make us cautious about our interpretations, humble in our approach to students and parents, and unwilling to take ourselves too seriously. It is not only students who see through the glass dimly, but teachers as well. Therefore, our conclusions about students and the learning environment are imperfect. While this reality need not undermine our assurance or authority, it does keep us constantly examining our practices, our motives, and our responses to what others say and do as a result of our teaching. It reminds us of our dependent status, and it should cause us to marvel that God and others treat us as well as they do—a sign of true humility (Stott 1978).

We must also be reminded that we too are seeking security, and that we cannot find it in the performance of our students, in their acceptance of us, or in the ratings of evaluators. Success with our students can easily become idolatry, and we may actually be performing well as teachers more to meet our own need to be loved and accepted than to meet our students' needs. Or at times, we may be more concerned about how well we are doing as teachers than we are about what is happening to our students. And the more time we spend being concerned about what we are doing, the less time we have to be concerned about what the students are doing—an illustration of true self-centeredness.

A Renewed Relationship and Standing with God

The wonder of redemption is that what was broken is being healed. What was wrong is being turned right. What was placed under a curse is being freed. What received judgment and death is receiving life. In other words, the effects of the fall are being reversed (Pratt 1979). God is fulfilling His original purposes for us and the creation in spite of our sin.

Through Jesus Christ, God has restored His image in the teacher, giving renewed standing, reissuing the call to witness to His character in our work as teachers, and empowering us to live out that calling. We live with our own weaknesses and sins, but we are not ruled by them any longer. We are able to discern the truth and the ways in which it should be taught. The Spirit of God also enables us to work out our beliefs creatively and effectively. In short, God enables us to do what He has called us to do as He walks with us, shedding His light on our paths, day by day and moment by moment. How simple, and yet how wonderful, that He enables us to be what we were created to be—something that those who do not bow to His claims on their lives search for in vain.

Jesus' death on the cross has released those whose faith is placed in Him from the condemnation of God (Romans 8:1). The sinful nature is crucified (Galatians 5:24), and we are set free from our enslavement to sin (John 8:34, 36; Romans 6:18, 22). Having put off the old self and its deceitful desires and practices, we have put on a new self that is being renewed in true righteousness and holiness (Ephesians 4:22, Colossians 3:9) to reflect the true image of the Creator. Human beings in Christ are new creatures (2 Corinthians 5:17), now able to be what they were created to be. Indeed, the change in our standing could not be more dramatic—from death to life, from unrighteousness to righteousness, from brokenness to wholeness, from enslavement to freedom.

The human being's standing with God is not the only relationship that has been altered. Redemption is cosmic in scope (Walsh and Middleton 1984), and therefore the whole creation will be restored (Matthew 19:28). Paul noted that the entire creation waits to "be liberated from its bondage to decay" (Romans 8:19–21), and several passages indicate that God will restore everything (2 Peter 3:10–13, Revelation 21:1, Acts 3:21). He will reconcile all things to Himself (Colossians 1:20) and "bring all things in heaven and on earth" under the headship of Jesus (Ephesians 1:10). Nothing created will escape His notice and the impact of redemption. All of creation exists in a different relationship as a result of the Cross.

While the kingdom of God has not been fully and completely established at this point in history, it has been inaugurated, and things are not what they were before (Luke 4:18–21). We still battle with sin and the old nature that is within us, but as with D-Day during World War II, the decisive battle has been won, in this case at the Cross. The day will come (V-Day) when the war is over and kingdom authority will be fully established (1 Corinthians 15:24). Until that day we live as residents of two kingdoms, one whose ruler is doomed to destruction and one whose ruler will reign forever (Anderson 1987).

Now What?

What dimensions of your created, fallen, image-bearing self seem to be prominent in dealing with your identified students? What is the impact, both positive and negative, on those students? What dimensions might be missing, or what would you like to change?

5 Teachers as New Creations

Most of us would like to think we are beyond the time of life when people ask, "Who am I?" That seems to be the question of adolescence. But there is a sense in which that question must always be kept before us, for the answer should guide and shape all that we do. If we lose sight of who we really are, it is most likely that we will begin to drift into thought and behavior that reflect a significant distortion of who God made us to be and what our faith in Christ means to us. So where do we start to answer that question?

An Identity Rooted in the Radical Grace of Jesus

To attach grace to our *identity* is a most significant thing. As we shall see, grace completely alters our understanding of who we are.

The grace of Jesus is radical, unlike anything else we have seen or known. When the very nature of grace is to give people the opposite of what they deserve, we know we are dealing with a most unusual, and probably threatening, entity. It simply does not fit any of the categories we normally use to manage the world. But the term *radical* does not just imply something different. In its various definitions in the *New Oxford American Dictionary* (Oxford University Press 2005), we find the following:

- "Relating to or affecting the fundamental nature of something; far-reaching or thorough"

- "Forming an inherent or fundamental part of the nature of someone or something"
- "Characterized by departure from tradition; innovative or progressive"
- "Advocating thorough or complete political or social reform; representing or supporting an extreme section of a political party"

Some of the descriptors used in the *Oxford American Writer's Thesaurus* (Lindberg 2004) include the following:

- "*Radical reform* THOROUGHGOING, thorough, complete, total, comprehensive, exhaustive, sweeping, far-reaching, wide-ranging, extensive, across the board, profound, major, stringent, rigorous. ANTONYM superficial."
- "*Radical differences between the two theories* FUNDAMENTAL, basic, essential, quintessential; structural, deep-seated, intrinsic, organic, constitutive. ANTONYM minor."
- "*A radical political movement* REVOLUTIONARY, progressive, reformist, revisionist, progressivist; extreme, extremist, fanatical, militant, diehard, hardcore. ANTONYM reactionary, moderate, conservative."

In other words, to describe the grace of Jesus as *radical* is to say not only that it is *different* but also that the *grace of Jesus is at the root of everything*; it is the very core of life, the most fundamental part of our existence. Nothing in life can be understood apart from the grace of Jesus. What we think, what we believe, what we do—everything must be infused with the grace of Jesus. If grace does not touch all, it is not the grace of Jesus.

The implication is that if we are followers of Jesus, when someone sees what flows from the very core of our existence, he or she should see grace alive. He or she should experience grace from our hands and mouths—especially in the moments when we are off guard. But of course, we cannot give it to others unless it truly is the most fundamental part of our own existence. There is no way it can ooze from our being to others unless we continue to drink afresh of Jesus' cup of grace each day and each moment. Our ability to give that grace to someone else depends directly on how much of it we have received ourselves. Little grace given means little grace received. Much grace received means much grace will be given. That suggests some things for us as teachers.

First, we must face and accept our own sin, our shortcomings, and our limitations as teachers. We cannot rest in "being right" all the time. While we may know more than our students, the reality is that we are just as fallen as they are and just as dependent on grace each day as they may be. We cannot receive grace apart from knowing how frail and wrecked by sin we are. This would lead us to readily confess both our weaknesses and our wrongdoings when appropriate and to not think more highly of ourselves than we ought. Examining our own hearts at the beginning of the day, during the day, and at the end of the day is a good way to be reminded of just how much the grace of Jesus carries us every moment of the day. We cannot really know the reality of grace apart from knowing and owning the reality of our own sin. Heart-level knowledge of the two is inseparable.

But living in grace is not just about being thankful for the forgiveness of sin. Jesus' grace is also about the freedom to live the abundant life—a radically different life. Jesus' grace gives us the freedom to take risks, to trust people, to think creative thoughts, to reach into places where others would not dare to go, to reach people others would not dare try to reach, to be happy, and to be sad and full of sorrow. It allows us to experience emotion. It allows us to love without expectation of something in return. It allows us to live at right angles to nearly everything that the world, our own flesh, and the devil tell us is the norm. An infusion of grace allows us to live fully like Jesus Himself. Go back to the definitions of *radical* stated earlier and see that the grace of Jesus is so radical that our whole lives should be lived very differently.

Grace is also disruptive. Anyone who is willing to go there, though, must realize that living by the grace of Jesus is also very *disruptive*. After all, if we are going to be that different and buck all the influences of "sound" thinking around us, we are not only going to be made uncomfortable ourselves, but we will make those around us uncomfortable too. This also must shape our understanding of who we are.

The grace given by Jesus was *very* disruptive, especially to the religious establishment and those who thought they were doing things as they should. Those who behaved the best, kept the rules the best, and maintained a generally spotless image before all onlookers actually resisted His grace and claimed that it was unrighteous and ungodly. They were outraged, and they fought against it.

Grace comes alive when things go wrong, when people mess up, when fairness does not seem to prevail. When everything is clean, neat, and tidy and students are well behaved and they do what we ask them to do, grace does not show up—it stays home, asleep. When I, as a teacher, have everything under control and things go as I want, I have no need of grace, and I will therefore also never show any—why would I need to? The rule of law is quite sufficient to keep things smooth—on the surface.

If grace shows up and takes over, it will first have to upset everything else that so effectively, but so falsely, "keeps the lid on." When I am safe and comfortable in all the ways I manage things in my life, grace is not necessary. When grace becomes the root of my existence, I had better watch out—life is about to be turned upside down.

Because of the nature of grace, people will not get what they deserve; they will get something much better. When I see others get something better than they deserve, I object because it is not justice, and it is not fair. After all, the way things are supposed to work is that people get what they deserve or what they earn. When I work hard to earn favor from God or others, I expect to receive it. I have fulfilled my part of the contract, and it is time for God to fulfill His. If I have not earned His favor, I will very likely want to offer an excuse to allow me to escape the consequences of what I deserve. In either case, it is a "do this and get that" mentality. I may want justice for others and hope to escape justice for myself, but in either case, the operational worldview is one of law and justice rather than mercy and grace. When events do not happen that way, I become unnerved since life is not working the way it is supposed to.

Grace may also confront me with the reality of just how bad I can be, a rather disconcerting thought for a person who had always been viewed as the "good boy." For me, that realization came during a particularly dark spiritual time in life when I had concluded that God did not care about me so I no longer cared about Him. I had told Him to forget it all. As one who had always been known for self-control, I found myself becoming so angry with others that at one point I know that if I had possessed a weapon I very likely could have beaten someone to death, a shocking realization for "Mr. Self-Control" but one that came at a time when I did not care anyway. What was I then to do when it was apparent that God blessed me in ways and circumstances that only He could have done? I could not even manage to *resist* Him as I had so carefully determined I would do!

You see, grace comes alive and becomes visible when the normal mode of operation is challenged and disrupted. I do something bad, and instead of the expected and deserved punishment I am given favor. My new self in Christ will receive that grace with joy and thanksgiving, but my flesh does not want to receive it—I want to believe that I have *earned* God's favor and approval.

Grace restores us as sons and daughters. We are no longer orphans, fugitives, or hired servants. If I am an orphan, that means I have no one to protect me, to be an advocate for me, to provide for me, to treasure me or delight in me, to bless me or walk with me on the journey. No one knows who I am or cares. I am nameless, rootless, of no value—a castaway.

If I am a fugitive, I am guilty and on the run, trying to not get caught. No place is safe for me; I cannot rest anywhere. I cannot be a part of or contribute to anything stable or long-term since I might be found out. I have to hide my identity lest I be turned in. If I am caught, it is all over.

If I am a hired servant, there are conditions that I must fulfill in order to be cared for. I must do what is required, or I will not be fed. I must not make mistakes, or my "contract" may be in jeopardy and I may get tossed out. If I perform beyond expectations, I may get a bonus, and if I do not perform as well as expected, I may take a cut in pay and benefits. All that I receive, I must earn.

The Bible tells us that by faith we are *beloved children of God*—not any old children but the children of a King who rules over all. What is life like for the child of a king? Everyone knows that the son or daughter of a king is very special. The whole kingdom rejoices over the birth of a prince or a princess. This child has access to everything in the king's castle. This child is the delight of the king, and he or she will inherit not only all the king's material goods but also his authority to rule. There is no doubt about his or her identity, and home is the safest place on earth. And the prince or princess does not have to earn his or her keep. By birthright, everything belongs to the child of a king.

The way we live reveals our deepest answer to the question of identity—as orphans, fugitives, hired servants, sons, or daughters. It reveals the way we have answered the great "identity" question. What do our lives say? If we live as orphans, fugitives, and hired servants, we do not know much about the restorative grace of Jesus. If we live as sons or daughters, the delight of the King's life, we have opened our hands and hearts to receive the grace that Jesus so doggedly continues to offer us.

Grace sets us free to live out the image of God placed within us. God makes it very clear that we are created in His image. That means when others look at us they are supposed to see a reflection of God—His character, His love, His very being. It is not the case that some of us have this image and others do not. What matters is the extent to which, and the direction in which, we live it out. That is determined by the degree to which we experience the freedom given to us through the grace of Jesus.

At the time of the fall, Adam and Eve did not lose the image of God; what they lost was the freedom and ability to live it out the way God intended. When the Bible says Jesus came to restore that which was lost, it does not mean to merely save lost people. It means to renew and to empower people to live out what God created them to be.

Apart from faith in Christ, we are limited to what we can muster out of our own gifts and determination. We are truly bound to the old self, the flesh. That is all we have from which to produce our efforts. Receiving the grace of Jesus in faith means we are no longer bound to those limits. We are now free to be what God created us to be and are empowered to do so through the living presence of the Holy Spirit.

We can again explore in awe and wonder the rest of creation. We can also rule over it (exercise dominion) with care and sensitivity and gratitude. We can love one another in trust and without fear. We can succeed or fail and all the while know that God has only good in mind for us. We can risk, we can invest, we can sacrifice, and we can live in reckless abandon and utter confidence, for we know that God is our all in all.

Security in the Intimate Love of the Father

The second great question in life is "Will I be OK?" First, Adam and Eve lost their identity and experienced shame in their being, and then they had to deal with being cast out of the garden—their place of ultimate security. Though it was clearly a result of their own doing, it was, nevertheless, a wound from the one with whom they had previously been completely united. God is the one who sent them away and banished them from returning; and God was the one who placed the curse on the earth, their work, Eve's childbearing, and the nature of their relationship with each other (Genesis 3).

While God can in no way be "blamed" for what happened, it still is hard for the now-fallen human beings, with their distorted perceptions, to believe that God could be trusted to not hurt them again. When the serpent tempted them to question whether God *really* had their best interests at heart, they gave in to the fear that perhaps He did not. I personally believe (though I know there are those who would differ with me) that their original sin was the sin of fear and lack of trust more than an angry act of rebellion. Anger and rebellion stem from fear, and fear stems from a lack of a true understanding and experience of love. Adam and Eve were unwilling to trust God when things were perfect. As fallen humans, their lack of trust in God's love and care for them would be even more evident. And if a lack of trust is how the break in relationship began, a restoration of trust is the only way the break will be healed.

God, in His infinite grace and mercy, even as He pronounced that they would be cut off, gave the promise that this would not be the end. He would not abandon them but would send one to redeem them and all the earth. But is it easy to trust someone who sent you away from home? I think not, even when He shows you many evidences of His continued love and care for you and even when He continues to invite you to come home to be with Him again.

We have undoubtedly inherited this problem. We are born into this world with a broken relationship with the one who has known our inmost parts since before we existed. We are born into a life of fear, innately sensing that we were abandoned at birth by the one who says He loves us. As we grow up, we learn to navigate and manage the world on our own, much like Cain, who as a fugitive and wanderer built himself a city (for security) and named it after his son (to establish an identity). We try to manage the world on our own because we are not sure that God will manage it to make us safe. In spite of how many times we are told and how many evidences we have seen, we are not sure we can trust God to have our best interests at heart. It is in our DNA from Adam and Eve. And as fallen people, we surely need *someone* to have our interests at heart.

Invited to come home. Our resistance and inability to trust God must surely break His heart just as Adam and Eve's resistance and inability to trust Him did; but He is not thwarted now, just as He was not then. His desire for us and His pursuit of us are relentless. His invitation for us to trust Him and to return "home," though it is no longer to Eden, is sincere and ongoing. He longs for His children to come home.

> Today the heart of God is an open wound of love. He aches over our distance and preoccupation. He mourns that we do not draw near to him. He grieves that we have forgotten him. He weeps over our obsession with muchness and manyness. He longs for our presence.
>
> And he is inviting you—and me—to come home, to come home to where we belong, to come home to that for which we were created. His arms are stretched out wide to receive us. His heart is enlarged to take us in.
>
> For too long we have been in a far country: a country of noise and hurry and crowds, a country of climb and push and shove, a country of frustration and fear and intimidation. And he welcomes us home: home to serenity and peace and joy, home to friendship and fellowship and openness, home to intimacy and acceptance and affirmation.
>
> We do not need to be shy. He invites us into the living room of his heart, where we can put on old slippers and share freely. He invites us into the kitchen of his friendship, where chatter and batter mix in good fun. He invites us into the dining room of his strength, where we can feast to our heart's delight. He invites us into the study of his wisdom, where we can learn and grow and stretch ... and ask all the questions we want. He invites us into the workshop of his creativity, where we can be co-laborers with him, working together to determine the outcomes of events. He invites us into the bedroom of his rest, where new peace is found and where we can be naked and vulnerable and free. It is also the place of deepest intimacy, where we know and are known to the fullest. (Foster 1992, 1–2)

The invitation is there; the question is whether we can trust Him enough to accept it and step onto the porch and through the door or whether fear will prevent us from going in. Not surprisingly, since fear and lack of trust were the problems in the beginning, they are still the problems now. But we must return home to Him if the wound is to be healed. And we must spend time with Him at home if we are to discover the fullness of the delight He takes in us. We will never know that His home is a safe place until we live there for a while.

It is significant to realize that home is a real *place*. We know that God is with us everywhere, but if we relate to Him *only* in the duties and responsibilities of ordinary life we are likely to miss something very important in His rebuilding of our relationship with Him and His healing of the wound. I have come to believe in the significance of special places where I go to meet with my Father—places that are for that purpose only.

They are places where I know that any distractions will be unlikely, where we can be alone and uninterrupted—sort of like the places I found when I was dating my future wife! They were *our* places, where the conversations led to a deeper intimacy. Deciding on such places to meet with God for special conversations is even more important.

I suggest that if we want to know the *intimate* love of the Father, this will be a common approach to prayer for us. And if we want to *live* in that intimate love, we will often return home to Him this way in prayer. This is what gives us the ultimate sense of security and answer to the question "Will I be OK?"

Living in Dynamic Fellowship with the Holy Spirit

The third big question in life is "What am I to be about?" If I can find my identity in Christ and my security in the Father's unfailing love for me, what then am I to do in life? All who claim to be followers of Jesus want to know God's will for their lives. We read books about discerning God's will, we pray that God will show us His will, we consult counselors and wise people to help us discern God's will for ourselves, and yet we seem quite uncertain as to just what it is and whether we are in it. Maybe we do not understand our relationship with the Holy Spirit very well.

We are partners with the Spirit. When Paul closes his second letter to the Corinthians with the words "May the grace of the Lord Jesus Christ, and the love of God, and the fellowship of the Holy Spirit be with you all" (2 Corinthians 13:14), just what does he mean by the *fellowship of the Holy Spirit*? My inquiry into the biblical meaning of the word *fellowship* suggests that there is a "doing" or "participating in something" together—a real partnership between the people involved. This partnership is a *dynamic* one in which both partners are active and involved, and each responds to the other's movement. Together they create something neither would do alone—it is better, more complete, and more lasting, and it has more impact.

Jesus told us that the Spirit would come to actually *reside in us*! That is indeed a pretty close relationship. Jesus said the Spirit would be our source of understanding, truth, light, life, and comfort. But when He speaks of *fellowship* with the Spirit, it cannot mean we become zeros in the relationship or in the work, the joy, the play, and the worship.

Perhaps we can liken the relationship to the one between two partners on the ballroom dance floor. One leads (the Spirit) while the other follows (us), but both are moving together and creating an act of grace and beauty. In order for this to happen, several things must take place. We could look at human dance to instruct us in the process of learning to dance with the Spirit.

First, there is an *experienced dancer who leads*, and we must not confuse the leader and the dancer. There is discussion about what the dance steps look like, then there is a demonstration, and finally the dancer actually participates in the act. Often the first attempts are somewhat clumsy. The dancer may step on the leader's foot, stumble, get tired and want to quit, or think the whole thing is hopeless. But the leader does not let the dancer quit; rather he engages the dancer in the discipline of the hard work it takes to learn the dance well. They rehearse over and over again until the steps become second nature to the dancer. But again, it is the leader who prompts it all and sets things into motion. Do we as teachers really behave as if the Holy Spirit leads like that in our classrooms?

There is also *rhythm* to a dance, and the leader again shows the dancer what the rhythm looks like. But the dancer must again step into the rhythm herself. There is a time to step and a time to hesitate. In the music itself, there is a time when the note is played and a time when there is silence and a rest. The rhythm of the music and the movement create something beautiful, something in which both the dancers and those who observe find grace and peace and wholeness. It is an act of *shalom*, in which things are as they were meant to be. Shalom involves a rhythm of action and rest, just as dancing does and just as teaching does. Teachers who do not understand this are subject to burnout and anger, or apathy and anger. The classroom is anything but a dance floor to them.

Finally, a dance is often an act of *celebration*. The dance may exist in order to celebrate some particular event, such as a wedding. But experienced dancers dance because the act itself is a celebration of life and a picture of true *fellowship*. It is also often an act that lovers engage in to express their oneness in dance. Such is worthy of a true celebration. The Holy Spirit is always celebrating the presence and existence of our students, and of us, the teachers. Do we fully participate in that celebration?

Now What?

In which area or areas described in this chapter would you say you desire to grow the most? How might that growth affect your interaction with your chosen students?

6 The Calling of a Teacher

Calling should not be thought of simply in terms of a career; it is more than that. Calling has to do with living out the particulars of who God made you to be in whatever context He may have placed you. For a Christian teacher who is working in the context of a public school, it is not being an evangelist or even a missionary. After all, you are primarily there to teach. It is, however, being "missional," in that you live out the truth of the gospel where you are and reveal both the kingdom and the heart of Jesus.

Revealing the Reality of the Kingdom

Perhaps it is inappropriate to say that our calling has somehow been *renewed*. The calling and task of humankind as originally decreed by God has never changed. What has changed is our ability and desire to fulfill that calling in a godly way. We have never ceased to fulfill our roles as children of God—acting to have dominion over the earth, or exercising faith, for example. Our approach since the fall has been to fulfill that role in an unrighteous and a perverted way. However, the call is being *reissued* to redeemed human beings who are now able to comprehend it and do something about it through the power of God's Spirit.

The focus of the calling, as has always been the case, is imitating God—in both a creative and a redemptive way. "In the final analysis, God's action in Christ ... culminates in Redemption. It is this action that we who are the New Humanity must seek to imitate as God's image-bearers in the world" (Anderson 1987, 128). Such a thought has manifold implications for the redeemed, both as individuals and as a corporate body.

As individuals, we are called to the imaging task as ministers of reconciliation through forgiving sin, healing brokenness, and restoring God's rule to every area of life. This is the heart of Jesus, and it reveals what the kingdom is about. As individuals, we are called to make a difference in the world, not just in our private, personal behavior. We are also called to the restoration task as communities of believers. Paul writes to churches (communities of believers) when he speaks of renewal (Ephesians 4:7–16, 22–24, 5:1–2; Colossians 3:5–17), indicating that the redemptive task that should be exhibited in our culture is not simply the work of individuals. Culture forming in a godly way is truly a communal task (Walsh and Middleton 1984).

There are several ways in which our behavior as redeemed image bearers should make a difference in the culture (Anderson 1987). Let's examine a few of them:

Healing. As healing, redemptive activity includes undoing the evil effects of the fall. Sickness, pain, suffering, and death came as part of the curse. It is our task, individually and corporately, to pursue righteous means of reducing sickness, pain, suffering, and death. This may mean physiological sickness, psychological suffering, intellectual emptiness, or spiritual death. Thus, we are not limited to the work of the medical profession. We are challenged as individuals and communities of believers to do something about the economic conditions that produce suffering, the social conditions that produce isolation and loneliness, the academic conditions that produce empty frustration, and the churches that do not produce life.

Reconciliation. As reconciliation, redemptive activity is the removal of the enmity, distortion, and disharmony brought on by the fall. Reconciliation should occur in our broken marriages and personal relationships, at work and in our neighborhoods, even internationally. Our redemptive activity should remove the enmity between different Christian groups and denominations. While Christ tells us that the world will know we belong to Him by the way we love one another in *unity*, all too often we display disharmony resulting from petty disagreements over trivial matters. Imaging God in our new nature will cause us to emit harmony.

Renewal. As renewal, redemptive activity involves more than just a return to a pre-fall paradise. All things will be made new in the final consummation of the kingdom, the heavenly city that far surpasses the garden. Renewal involves taking something that already exists and making something better of it. We should seek renewal in our cities, housing projects, corrupt governments, and industry that has so little concern for its workers. As Christians, shouldn't we be involved in creating schools that pursue the task God has given to us instead of the task a godless society has dictated? We are called to build something better that reflects the glory of God in its completion and operation just as the new heaven and the new earth will.

Deliverance. As deliverance, redemptive activity should remove us and others from the bondage prevailing in the kingdom of darkness. Manifold powers seem to rule over us—poverty, drugs, sexual immorality, racial oppression. Image-bearing activity will lead us to attempt (through God's power) to break the rule that such things have over the lives of people in our world. God did not sit back and say, "How awful, but that is just the way it is." Neither can those who seek to reflect who He is.

Justice. As justice, redemptive activity seeks to right those wrongs precipitated by the fall, especially those we inflict on one another. Is a legal system satisfactory when it allows criminals to avoid conviction on the basis of a procedural error? Is a legitimate business venture acceptable even if it depends on the exploitation of certain people? Should we be content with a school disciplinary system that metes out punishment without regard to the nature of the crime? A concern for justice must manifest itself in the way human beings deal with other human beings if we are to be faithful to our calling.

Peace. Peace expresses the state of what some might call living the "good life." The biblical term is *shalom*, which means "dwelling in harmony and peace with God, others, self, and the surroundings." It reflects the wholeness and togetherness God intended and not simply a cheap coexistence. This wholeness should be evident in our work, families, church life, and personal outlook on life. Our concern for the welfare of the environment as part of God's creation should keep us from simply using the environment for our own convenience. This same wholeness must keep us from being content to live our own lives, unconcerned for others as long as they do not harm us and we do not harm them.

We can readily see that our calling will not allow us simply to be content with souls that are saved and personal behavior that is ethical. God Himself identified with His people and came to them to live in their presence. The incarnation is a marvelous lesson in how we are meant to live out the image of God in the current age.

The school provides us with manifold opportunities to reveal what healing, reconciliation, renewal, deliverance, justice, and peace are to look like. We should expect it to be so, since what goes on in schools is a part of God's kingdom work.

Revealing the Heart of Jesus the Disciple Maker

We are not only called to reveal the nature of God's kingdom to a broken, watching world; we are also privileged and trusted to reveal the heart of Jesus. In a school setting, that can take many forms, but one important one has to do with making disciples of our students. Whatever else it may be, disciple making is a matter of the heart. So what is Jesus' heart toward those He disciples?

The eternal commitment of Jesus' heart. I believe it is important to realize that the commitment of Jesus to love, care for, save, lead, teach, and empower His disciples began in eternity and that it was first a commitment between the members of the Holy Trinity. It existed before there were any human beings to deserve or not deserve that commitment. It did not take long for Adam and Eve to become unworthy of that commitment, but God spelled it out plainly for them in Genesis 3. Life would be hard, things would not be as they were designed to be, Adam and Eve would physically die, but Jesus would honor the commitment and come to rescue them and their seed, in all their fear and against all their resistance. The commitment made by God could not be thwarted by the failure of His creatures to keep theirs.

What does God's commitment say to us as teachers? Unfortunately, being the fallen and finite people we are, all too often our commitment to our students is heavily determined by whether they can show they deserve it, or at least that they are trying to do and be what we ask of them. We expect them to fail often enough, but if they are not at least trying … If a failure to try had eliminated or even diminished Jesus' commitment to us, where would we be?

The implications seem pretty obvious, don't they? Our commitment to our students must begin long before we know who they are, and it must not be thwarted or diminished by how poorly they perform or behave or whether they fail to do the right thing. It cannot be enhanced by whether it appears that they might be successful and obedient and whether they seem, therefore, somehow more worthy of our commitment. It has to come from our living in the commitment that the triune God has made to us.

So what would that commitment look like? In what ways would our students experience that commitment from us? While it certainly involves working hard at all the normal tasks entrusted to a teacher, it is far more than working hard. It involves a heart that is ready to give itself away, knowing that it will be bruised and battered by some and warmly embraced by others. It involves a heart that knows its own broken condition and that is willing to entrust itself to other broken hearts—even students' hearts—all because it ultimately has entrusted itself to the broken and wounded heart of Jesus. It also involves a heart that is full of hope and that is given away to all, even when everything has gone wrong. It is a heart that is full of compassion and mercy and courage.

Giving our heart away by entrusting it to others who we know will bruise it or reject it is quite contrary to what many of us experience from and give to others. Most of us spend great energy guarding and protecting our hearts from being wounded by others.

Given our fears and sinfulness, that is understandable; but it is not the way of Jesus. It is not the way that evidences commitment to other broken hearts no matter what.

The ongoing investment of Jesus' heart. In the financial world, one takes what is sometimes hard earned, and at least always valuable, and invests it in a company or a project (always managed by human beings), with the hope and expectation that the investment will help the company grow to produce its goods, which are for everyone's good. (Well, at least in some companies that is true!) There is a choice involved, and although "smart" people choose companies that have a proven track record, we all know there are those also who take risks on the unknown. Sometimes investment in the unknown produces phenomenal results. Other times it produces abject failure and loss. Long-term investors who are not afraid and who hold a large supply of assets that will carry them through some losses are willing to risk and thus keep the market going and help shape progress in the economy and the society. They do not quit, even when there is a large loss. This type of investment takes a heart of courage.

Certainly all such analogies eventually break down, and I am not sure this is even a good one, but perhaps the point of this one helps us understand the ongoing investment that God makes in us. It is a courageous choice on His part; He has unlimited assets to carry Him through the failures and losses, He keeps investing, and He certainly takes risks on us. And as a result, He is building a kingdom of people who are able then to invest in others to reveal what He is like.

So what did the investment by Jesus in His disciples look like, and what might that mean for us as teachers? It may be important to notice that the first thing He did as He began to invest His heart and being in them was to call them away from the things they had invested their hearts in already. They were supposed to leave everything and follow Him wherever He went, listen to whatever He said, and do whatever He did. They had to put away all their preconceived notions of the way the world worked. What a creative opportunity that is for us as teachers! Is it possible that we as disciple makers are invited to or even expected to turn our students' worlds upside down and inside out by having them follow us as we follow Jesus? I think so.

Learning that lasts involves the resolution of a creative tension—a reduction of the dissonance between the way things are and the way they are supposed to be. And way back there in the beginning in Genesis 3, we see the promise of commitment being voiced, and at the same time we hear that things in the world will not operate as they were supposed to because of the image bearers' disobedience. So the fact that things are not the way they are supposed to be should not surprise us. The challenge for us is to turn that reality into learning!

But we cannot merely do so through lectures and papers and tests and other paper-and-pencil (or PowerPoint) activities. As teachers we must engage the world in redemptive ways, and we must invite and expect our students to go with us. We get to mentor them in the process. And we get to walk with them through the issues that matter to them, not just the ones that matter to us. Facing the challenge of things that matter to them that are not the way they are supposed to be is a step toward encouraging them to learn to give away their own hearts.

We must realize, though, that just as it did for Jesus, this process takes a heart of great courage. We and our students would always rather hide from the things that are not the way they are supposed to be, just as Adam and Eve did after they disrupted everything. Jesus was not afraid to expose the fearful, self-protective, foolish hearts of His disciples. He was not afraid to ask them to walk into situations that were beyond their control. He was not afraid to trust them with work that was beyond their human capacities. In fact, He sent them into those situations. But note also that when He sent the twelve or the seventy out to do impossible work, He empowered them to do it with His own Spirit. Is that not a creative challenge for us to figure out—how do we empower our students to leave the safe environs of our classrooms to go do the impossible task of changing things to resemble more of what they are supposed to be? And do we have the courage to face the results that our students might create? What an invitation from God to be a partner with Jesus!

The safe haven of Jesus' heart. If we take what I have just said seriously, we know we are in for many disappointments, painful failures, and in general, a messy learning situation. How are third graders going to attempt to change the world from what it is to what it should be? How are self-conscious and self-serving seventh graders going to give away what they are so desperately trying to protect—their hearts? How are high school seniors who have finally made it to the top of the heap going to step out to do the impossible and get their faces smashed and their confidence shredded? What in the world would make it safe for these students to have the courage to try to make a difference in the world, to actually try to live like Jesus?

Well, what in the world makes it safe for us to try that? What made it possible for Jesus' disciples to do so, even in the face of persecution and ultimately execution? I think that it is the infinite compassion of Jesus. His heart was always open to them, and it was safe for them to try and to fail. Even when rebuked, they knew they were safe with Him. He always received them, spoke into their lives as they needed Him to, saved them from disaster when necessary, picked them up after failure, and even forgave them for rejecting Him in fear when things got too tough and scary. "Come to me, all who are weary and heavy-laden, and I will give you rest" (Matthew 11:28, NASB). That is, Jesus is offering to His listeners a safe haven, especially when their weariness and burdens come as a result of their own "mess-ups."

Again, what are the implications for us as teachers? How do we provide a safe haven for our students? How do we have compassion on them? Our first mistake would be to think that such compassion means that we do not discipline them, correct them, or have expectations of them. Jesus did all those things, sometimes even in what must have been a tough voice. But He was so committed to them and He had invested Himself so much in them that they knew even His rebukes, His pointing out their lack of faith, and His over-the-top expectations were evidence of His love for them. And they knew that He always longed for them to come home to Him to find solace, to find mercy, to experience grace, and to receive His long-suffering compassion.

Academically, a heart of compassion could evidence itself in structuring assignments and examinations in a way that students are always invited and sometimes even expected to try and try again if first efforts produce unacceptable performance. A heart of compassion could mean using formative evaluations to enable a student to build his or her final product into a success. It means that the relationship between teacher and student is clearly independent of achievement.

Behaviorally, a heart of compassion could mean that systems of rewards and punishments do not define classroom discipline. It could mean that when a student is at his or her worst, the teacher responds with grace instead of law, the teacher reaches out with an open hand and heart to hear and console instead of with a closed fist and an angry heart ready to demand conformity.

In all areas of school life—athletics, academics, any cocurricular activities—it could mean that the atmosphere is one of cooperation and standing in the gap for those who are lacking rather than an atmosphere of competing, judging, winning, and losing. What really reveals redemption in a broken world more: a new school record in the 100-yard dash or a race in which the Special Olympics kids running the race see that one runner has fallen and they all return to pick up that runner and laughingly all join hands and cross the finish line together? (I realize that story could be apocryphal, but it makes the point.)

The confidence of Jesus' heart. How can I say that Jesus had a heart that was confident toward His disciples? Were they not dull in understanding, a dichotomous mixture of arrogant and fearful in challenging situations, lacking in faith, argumentative about who would be the greatest in the kingdom, inept in almost every way? Yes, they were. They did not have it together.

Yet Jesus left the earth and gave them the most important work in the universe to do. What a group to hand over your mission to! But then why should Jesus have been confident in anything regarding His earthly ministry at all? From a human point of view, even His work on earth appeared to be an utter failure.

Clearly, Jesus' confidence was not in anything earthly. It was in His Father and in the Spirit. Jesus knew what His Father was up to, and He knew that the Spirit would carry it out and finish what Jesus had started. Jesus knew that His work was finished but that the Spirit's was not. He also knew that His Father was in charge and that nothing could thwart the Father, including the sin and failure of the image bearers. Jesus knew that what appeared to be was not what was really going on.

I think these truths give us great confidence as teachers! Sometimes I think our theology of the Holy Spirit is much more advanced than our practice and experience of Him! We act as if what we do in the classroom and in a student's life determines what will become of that student. We act as if what is going on in the home or with peers is so powerful that it will determine what becomes of that student. We act as if our great lecture, creative lesson, clever insight, or whatever else we do right is supposed to make that student come out right. We act as if our mistakes will keep that student from making it in life.

Where is our confidence in the Holy Spirit as an active agent in the classroom and out of the classroom? Do we not know that whatever we do right in a student's life will have a desired, positive effect only as the Holy Spirit makes it so? Do we not think that the Spirit is active in overcoming our mistakes? Is it not the Spirit who enables us to even come close to dispensing grace to our students such that they have a living taste of what Jesus longs to give them?

Conclusion. I have tried to say that teachers are in the business of making disciples and that disciple making is a matter of the heart—a heart of commitment that never gives up, a heart of courage that invests, a heart of compassion that provides a safe haven, and a heart of confidence that believes in students because it believes in a God who is active in the lives of students and in the whole world. But of course, there is no way to make disciples without first being one. Jesus has this same heart toward you and me. Can we receive it and live close to it so that we can give it away to our students who need it?

Now What?

What does the idea of revealing the presence of the kingdom and the heart of Jesus suggest to you in your teaching? What does, or could, that look like—in general and specifically in regard to your chosen students?

Part 3

Understanding Our Students

7 God's Image in Learners: Part 1

Just as we must recognize the image of God in ourselves, so we must embrace it as the fundamental nature of our students, no matter how they behave or how many problems they may have. To fail to treat them as image bearers is a great insult to God, and it serves to reduce, if not destroy, them as human beings. The biblical doctrines of the creation, fall, and redemption form the basis for our understanding of the nature of the learner, so we will begin with a look at the "creation" dimension of the framework.

There is a difference between being like God and being God. God's attributes are infinite and perfect, but ours are finite by creation and imperfect because of the fall. Being finite and imperfect does not allow us to think that we can be less than the image, however. The reflection is not the real thing, but it shows what the reality looks like. So it is with us. We are not God, but as the image or reflection of God, we must show what the reality of God is like. As a reflection, we must then display the attributes of God in all dimensions of life as God enables us to do so. What, then, are the attributes of God that we should display, and how in our finite way do we display them?

Active and Purposeful

God's revelation of Himself begins in the early chapters of Genesis. Creation is a mighty act of God. Perhaps that goes without saying, but as we look at the reflection of God in our students, it is no small issue. God *does* things. He acts throughout the course of history, bringing creation into existence (Genesis 1–2), leading the Israelites out of Egypt (Exodus 5–14), and causing the rise and fall of kings (Exodus 9:16) and kingdoms (Habakkuk 1:5–11). Events do not just happen of their own accord; God makes them happen (Psalm 135:6).

Also, God does not make things happen at random. All things happen according to His will and good purpose (Ephesians 1:11). God is busy redeeming His people (2 Timothy 1:9) and doing all things to reveal His glory (Psalm 72:19, Revelation 4:11). Whether we understand all His actions or not, they serve to bring the course of history to a climax in the second coming of Christ. God's acts of mercy and judgment move the creation toward that glorious end.

While students reflect these attributes finitely and imperfectly, they are nonetheless called to reflect them (Genesis 1:26, Colossians 3:10, Ephesians 4:24). The educational process must be designed to help them learn to reflect these attributes in all of life's activity. School life and teachers' approaches can either enhance the development of these characteristics or hinder it. Understanding what these characteristics mean in human nature is important to ensuring enhancement.

Our students' actions are no less purposeful than God's. The purpose may be terribly self-centered or unacceptable to God (or other human beings), but there is a purpose of some kind. They find it necessary to understand reality in order to find a secure place in it, and they are constantly seeking to make sense of things in relation to themselves.

Common sense may tell us that a child who sits in the classroom doing nothing is a child with no purpose. A child who wanders aimlessly from task to task accomplishing little of significance to anyone else, or who cannot finish a task, is also seen as having no purpose. But nothing could be further from the truth. In fact, it is impossible to be made in God's image and be without purpose.

The purpose of such children may not match the purpose that we have for them, but children who are "doing nothing" or who may be acting up in the classroom are very actively controlling their own situation and placing themselves in the position that best seems to provide what they need—regardless of whether it *actually* meets those needs.

Children who cannot finish a task take each task to the point where they can remain in control and then stop. Stopping is exactly the way they maintain control. The rest of us think that since they quit they have no control, but the case is quite the contrary. This type of action, inadequate as it may be, is their way of finding themselves and their place in the scheme of things. It is their effort to put things in a perspective that they can handle.

Perhaps it is also important to say here that students' acting with purpose means that students are not simply conditioned by their environment or at the mercy of their genes. Both the environment and the genes play a significant role in their makeup and their behavior, but they do not control them. God does not hold the environment accountable for their behavior; He holds them accountable (Romans 1:20, 2:1). While God clearly formed them from dust (Genesis 2:7), He never deals with them as if they were only the product of chemical reactions. We must surely reject such reductionist views of human beings and the resulting approaches to behavior, learning, and education.

Rational

Just as creation was a mighty act, it was the act of a *mighty mind*—thinking, forming, and evaluating (Packer 1979). Rationality is a basic element in God's character as He holds things together through law and order (Genesis 8:22, Jeremiah 31:35–36). He operates reasonably and not chaotically (Genesis 1), and the world makes sense, even in all its sometimes seemingly unexplainable complexities. The thought that the world, in all its mystery, could have been created and then subsequently held together by chance is one of the most preposterous of our creative ideas concerning the nature of the universe.

In order to exercise any rule over the creation as God directed, our students must have the power of reason. Without it, the task could hardly be fulfilled in any satisfactory way. They find it necessary to perceive what is happening around them so that they can act. They conceptualize ideas and experiences in a fashion that makes sense to them. When things do not seem to make sense, they are at a loss as to how they should act. Such confusion often leads to paralysis—they simply do not know how to cope with a situation in which they can see no sensible order. But even paralysis is a use of their reasoning—their mind says that doing nothing is the smartest and safest thing to do.

I must hasten to add that they do not always perceive things in the way they *actually* exist, nor do they always act on the basis of true order (Romans 1:21–23). When we as teachers see them behave in accord with distortions, we often say that they have acted irrationally. While the behavior may be irrational from our perspective (or even God's), it is perfectly rational to them as they have put things together in their own way and acted accordingly.

This would be true of many of our students who come to school from such broken, and sometimes terrifying, backgrounds. Their responses appear irrational and very unhelpful to the rest of us. But because they carry the rational character of our Creator, what we consider to be distorted and ineffective is really the best they can produce and is what at the moment seems like the best way to make sense of things. It is their distorted use of the rational characteristic that was implanted in them by God.

When they perceive what is happening and relate it to themselves, place events in their own frameworks (systems of order), formulate ideas, and evaluate all these perceptions and events, they are engaging in that wonderful process called *thinking*. Such a statement would hardly suffice as a definition of thinking, but a definition is unnecessary to make the point. When we understand that students are made in the image of a rational, thinking God, we realize that they are thinking all the time. We can no longer allow ourselves to complain that our students just do not think, or know how to think. Thinking is woven into the fabric of our existence (Genesis 2:19). All their efforts to make sense of the world and to know how to respond to it involve thinking, but the thinking they do in coping with a given situation as God sees it may again be very distorted, inadequate, and ineffective.

Creative

Genesis 1 reveals God as the great Creator. He formed the universe in all its diversity and pronounced it "good" (Genesis 1:25). God seems to take delight not only in the works He created but also in telling about His work in some detail. To describe the work He performed day by day and to include discussion of everything from the sun and stars to the fish and creeping things indicates that creating was a significant activity for Him. It is no less significant for students who are to bear His image.

When God pronounced His creation *good*, He imparted value to it. As we make value judgments about our creations, we in a sense "declare" value also. Forming and imparting value are two dimensions of the creative character of God and thus of human beings (Packer 1979).

The pattern of laboring to produce something worthwhile and then delighting in it is certainly appropriate for our students. Their creativity is not restricted to making material things, however. All of life is seen as a creative act in which they use their minds, their emotions, their wills—their entire being—to form and utilize concepts and material things.

An artist (a creative person) is a passionate person who feels deeply the tragedy and beauty of life; who appreciates shapes, sounds, and textures; and who selects and molds thoughts and materials with a sense of excitement about being involved. Does this not also characterize God? Why, then, shouldn't this passion characterize a human being's approach to all of life? Moses and Elijah were passionate men, the psalmist certainly appreciated beauty, and Paul was deeply involved in action, using his knowledge and emotion in creative ways as he instructed and ministered to both Jew and Gentile (Macaulay and Barrs 1978).

While God created out of nothing, students are certainly limited in their creative capacities by their finiteness and their dependence on God. However, they are not only *capable* of creating manifold things and ideas, they are actually *called* to do so in order to be God's partners in managing the creation (Genesis 1:26). People create works of art, books, scientific theories, philosophies, bridges, airplanes, films, and even families. All facets of culture have been created through our working with what God has created and placed in the universe, whether physical things or conceptual truth. We are inevitably busy in the work of forming the culture and our lives in it. Students, however limited by developmental capacity and magnitude of learning, are called to do the same.

Students are also constantly making value judgments about the new ideas they apply to situations or the things they create with their own hands. They decide what is good or bad and what is worth keeping, and they decide what to appreciate. By God's design, this evaluation of their creations should delight them, both in the product or idea that they have created and in the process they use to create it. Such an evaluation also, in a sense, imparts value to their creations. Again, we see them acting like God.

It is apparent, though, that their creative capacity and their ability to perform the same function as God are not always put to godly use. Cain and Lamech are early examples of the perverted use of the creative image (Genesis 4:16–24). Cursed by God to be a wanderer and fugitive for the rest of his life, Cain left and created a city. Why would a fugitive create a city and then name it after his son? Fugitives have no security and can have no stable identity. If their true identity is discovered, their lives are apt to be cut short. They must stay on the move and hide their identity.

However, no one can live that way for long, and Cain was no exception. He created a city of his own for security and named it after his son to strengthen his sense of identity. Indeed, he created. He used his image power, but he created with the wrong motives, with the wrong ends in mind, and apart from the pleasure of God. And while Lamech created much more (his children raised livestock, played the harp and flute, and forged all kinds of tools), Lamech's pleasure was short-lived, as his value judgments were centered only on himself (demonstrated by his statement that if Cain were to be avenged seven times then Lamech seventy-seven times—Genesis 4:24). His world was entirely self-centered.

Unfortunately, we as teachers can also act in a fashion that tends to deny the characteristic of creativity and that may hinder its development and use in others. This travesty is often at its worst in schools. A child's creativity is often squelched before the second grade. Since so much schoolwork is geared toward finding the "correct" answer, students sometimes find it unsafe to engage in any creative thinking. Creative responses often do not conform to the expected standards or traditions, and they are therefore threatening. The need for security and stability seems to put tremendous pressure on any nonconformity. To be safe and secure, students must all be alike and follow the acceptable norms. Such pressure diminishes the opportunity to be creative and often extinguishes it altogether. In creating this pressure, we deny the image of God in them and reduce our troubled students to something less than fully human.

For broken students who use their creativity in destructive, self-protective, hurtful ways, it is even harder for teachers to tap into that creativity in a fruitful way. Most often our response will be to trample their creativity in order to stop the destruction and hurt. Instead of redirecting their creativity, we tend to want to kill it.

Moral

In the issue of morality, God's character sets the standard for right and wrong. As He has revealed Himself to humankind in His Word and His Son, He has revealed what is right—"to love mercy" (Micah 6:8), to heal (Psalm 147:3), to "hate evil" (Psalm 97:10), to be selfless (Philippians 2:5–8). Anything that goes against His character is wrong. We are to judge our own actions precisely by that standard.

God's actions throughout history have also set the standard for justice. While we cannot read God's mind in determining justice in a given situation, He has given us much information about His sense of justice through the record of His dealings with His people. Our actions in executing justice for others must be guided by His actions and His teachings concerning justice. An individual approach to standards for justice, or even a common consent approach, leads only to eventual frustration and confusion. In our sinful state, we can hardly be expected to arrive at a workable system of justice that will be acceptable to all humankind, let alone to God. Someone higher than we are must provide the basis for justice.

Adam was created as a moral creature and was righteous through his obedience to God's commands. But because he chose to disobey God so that he might know good and evil, he became unrighteous (Romans 5:19). He did not become amoral, however. As Adam's descendants, we still have a sense of right and wrong, and all our acts are either righteous (in accordance with God's norms) or unrighteous (contrary to God's norms). We choose between right and wrong (Psalm 119:30), and our actions display the direction of our choices and thus our hearts (Mark 7:21).

Different systems of morality exist in various cultures, but all cultures have some such system. Students constantly make judgments about their own actions and the actions of others. Their actions tend to bring about justice or injustice. If they act in accordance with principles derived from God's actions, they tend to bring about justice. That means, of course, that there is no acceptable standard but God's standard. God's law is our loving guide in applying justice, and all people are expected "to act justly" (Micah 6:8) and thus again to reflect God's character. As we will see later, redemption has made it possible for us to once again act in "true righteousness and holiness" (Ephesians 4:24), and as Christian teachers we must.

Free and Responsible

God acts freely according to His own purposes, making choices to do as He will. He is certainly accountable to no one, but He cannot act in contradiction to Himself and His own standards. To apply such characteristics to human beings, some adjustments must be made, but we shall see that the Scriptures help us do just that.

God decides how He will direct the course of history, but it is interesting to note how many references to God's choices involve choosing people. The Lord chose the people of Israel and set His affection upon them (Deuteronomy 7:6–7), not because of any inherent attractiveness or power they possessed but simply out of His own will. The nation He chose for His inheritance (Psalm 33:12) received His blessing, indicating that *He chooses for the purpose of bringing about good*. He chose His people "from the beginning" (2 Thessalonians 2:13), before the foundation of the world (Ephesians 1:4), before they could do anything to sway His judgment—a clear indication that His choices are indeed of His own free will. While only God is free in the sense of being totally self-determining, we are also free within the limits of our finiteness. That is part of God's image in us. We are able to make choices within the limits of the nature that God gave us. Such must not be denied to our students.

Moses exhorts God's people to choose life rather than death so that they and their children might live and love the Lord their God (Deuteronomy 30:19–20). Joshua tells the people to choose whom they will serve (Joshua 24:15). Proverbs contains numerous exhortations to choose the right things, indicating our ability to do so. Among those exhortations are to choose God's instruction (8:10) and understanding (16:16). John 7:17 tells of choosing "to do God's will."

When students submit themselves to God, they are truly free as they live out the nature that God gave them. When they deny God, they lose their true freedom and settle for something less than what they really are. They still make choices and are held accountable for those choices, and they are still human whether they are living as such or not. Again, history is full of people who made wrong choices, with many of those choices recorded in the Scriptures. In the beginning God gave a command to Adam and Eve that they chose to disobey (Genesis 2:16–17, 3:6).

The evidence of Adam's faulty choice has been readily visible in all human beings ever since (Romans 1:19–32).

That God holds human beings accountable for their choices seems irrefutable. We will reap the consequences of our choices, whatever they may be. The death of David and Bathsheba's infant son is a profound example (2 Samuel 12:11–18). Other Scriptures supporting this same idea are Proverbs 11:18, 22:8; Job 4:8; Hosea 8:7, 10:12; 2 Corinthians 9:6; and Galatians 6:7–8.

Freedom and responsibility go hand in hand, and to accept one without the other leads to distortion and disruption. God gave us the capacity to choose and the responsibility to do so. Our duty, then, is to live up to the responsibility to make the choices and then to accept the responsibility for them. The educational process must again provide the opportunity for students to make choices and live with the consequences of those choices. Teaching is not simply telling people what to believe and do.

Faithful

Faithfulness is another important characteristic of God. To be faithful is to know the truth, to be committed to it, and to act in accordance with it. As God is the author of truth, He cannot act in contradiction to His commitment to the truth, whether it is a commitment to what is right or a commitment to His people. Every act of God is an act of His faithfulness.

The Scriptures contain countless references to God's faithfulness. Moses says God is "a faithful God who does no wrong" (Deuteronomy 7:9, 32:4). "The Lord is faithful to all His promises" (Psalm 145:13) and "remains faithful forever" (146:6). We see God's commitment to His people in the way that He doesn't let us be tempted beyond what we can bear (1 Corinthians 10:13) and in His strengthening and protecting us from the evil one (2 Thessalonians 3:3).

As we seek to apply this attribute to our students, we encounter some difficulties. Because of the fall, they are not faithful in the sense that God is. Nevertheless, this part of the image is still with them, albeit in a distorted way (like all other characteristics after the fall). It might be more accurate to describe them as *faith-full*, meaning that they are creatures of faith who make commitments to something as truth and then act in accordance with those commitments—be they right or wrong. When the Scriptures describe human beings as faithless, that does not mean they exist with no faith at all, but rather that they have no faith in the true God. It is a case of bad faith rather than no faith.

For human beings are inherently religious beings, having faith in something and in some god, even if it is a god of our own making (Walsh and Middleton 1984). We may indeed fashion a god and worship it (Isaiah 44:15), or we may worship the creatures rather than the Creator (Romans 1:21–25). In either case, we are revealing the need to be committed to something as a god and as the truth on which we can then base our actions. Again, this is as true of our students as it is us.

Students act on the basis of their beliefs, whether or not those beliefs correspond with reality. "A person will act on the basis of a false belief just as vigorously as he will act on the basis of a true belief. The child who believes that there is a ghost in his closet will cry just as loudly whether the belief is true or false. The important thing is the belief of the child, not the actual condition which prevails" (DeJong 1977, 34).

Students find security in the things they believe. They can do nothing apart from faith (believing something to be true), even if it is just sitting in a chair. As they seek answers to deeper questions about meaning in life, such as their origin and destiny or the nature and source of truth, they also exercise faith. And that faith cannot be only in the things that are seen. Those who would have us believe that truth comes only from scientific endeavor, which can be observed and measured, fail to realize the faith commitment they have already made to something that is unseen—the idea that all truth can be provided through science. We all do walk by faith (2 Corinthians 5:7), whether in things we see or in things we do not see. The exhortation is to walk by faith in God and truth as He has revealed it, not by faith in something less—another great challenge for the educational endeavor.

Now What?

As you consider your identified students, which image-bearing characteristics seem to be most evident in them, even if displayed in destructive ways? How could you focus on and encourage those characteristics in them?

8 God's Image in Learners: Part 2

God's Stewards

God, of course, rules sovereignly over all things (Psalm 135:5–7). There is nothing that He does not control, as He is the initiator and sustainer of all things that exist (Nehemiah 9:6). It may appear to us at times that things are out of His control, but if that were the case, God would not be God. Joseph was well aware of this fact (Genesis 50:19–20), but we struggle with it because we are simply unable to fully comprehend what is happening in a given situation. While evil may give us the most difficulty, the Scriptures indicate that God is even sovereign over evil (Job 2:10, Acts 4:27–28). God is not evil, nor does He manifest evil acts, yet He oversees and places limits on the work of the devil himself (Job 1:12).

God does not rule capriciously or selfishly. Rather, He rules purposefully, rationally, creatively, righteously, and lovingly (Psalms 104:24, 145:17). In short, ruling is a part of His nature that requires the use of all His other attributes. God rules in accordance with what He is, and we cannot do otherwise. Such a realization forces us to be concerned for the status of our hearts, "for as [a man] thinks in his heart, so is he" (Proverbs 23:7, NKJV). The way we exercise control over the world is determined by what is in our hearts.

As God's stewards, our students are to exercise a measure of control over the environment and the created things living in it (Genesis 2:15, 19–20).

Unfortunately, when their hearts are turned away from God, just the opposite is the case—the environment and created things control them. Such is the nature of any idolatry. When we worship what we have created, it is bound to rule us instead of the other way around (Romans 1:23–25). But when our hearts are right with God, we can respond purposefully, rationally, creatively, righteously, and lovingly to His call to exercise dominion. Anything less, and we do not adequately reflect the character of our Maker.

As we think of the various ways our students might be expected to rule, it is obvious that ruling involves developing a culture. This should be a very creative and purposeful act. We use our rational powers to create governments, aesthetic products, and all other dimensions of culture. In other words, just as God uses all His other attributes to rule the creation, our students are to do the same since they are His agents. The issue is not *whether* they will exercise control but *how* they will exercise it. They can do it righteously and lovingly so that the creative, rational, and purposeful nature of what they do will glorify God, or they can do it for their own glory. God's expectation is set clearly before them, but the accomplishment of the task depends on the condition of their hearts and the extent to which they *learn* to do those things that will fulfill His expectations. Such learning, then, is a primary concern for the educational process.

Social

Using the adjective *social* in describing God is probably using a human term to name a godly attribute. It makes more sense to say that God exists in a state of relationship and fellowship. God was a triune God before creation, and the three persons of the Godhead had fellowship with one another before human beings came on the scene. The idea of fellowship involves working together, sharing experiences, communicating with one another, and dwelling together in peace. Such is the case in the Godhead.

At creation we hear God say, "Let *us* make man in our image" (Genesis 1:26; emphasis mine), a statement not only of plurality of persons but also of joint effort— fellowship as we have defined it. In Genesis 11:7 God says, "Let *us* go down and confuse their language" (emphasis mine), another instance of the three persons of God acting together to accomplish something significant. In Isaiah 6:8 God asks, "And who will go for *us*?" (emphasis mine), now reflecting a desire for someone else to participate in the fellowship of the work of the Godhead.

It is clear that fellowship within the Godhead is not the only relationship God desires. His design for humankind reveals two other significant relationships: (1) God with human beings and (2) human beings with other human beings. That God desires a relationship with us is evident through His establishment of a covenant with us. As the sovereign King, God establishes a relationship with us that He defines by promising to protect, nourish, and deliver us as His part, and by stipulating faithfulness and obedience as our response. God bound Himself to us, and we are to obey and serve Him. Our obedience brings a blessing, and our disobedience brings a curse (Anderson 1987).

The covenant idea is not the only thing that indicates God's desire to be in fellowship with us, however. The Old Testament tells us of the fellowship offering (Leviticus 3:1, Numbers 15:8, Exodus 32:6), the only sacrifice that allowed the person offering the sacrifice to eat a part of it. Through this sacrifice the sinner had fellowship with God and the priest.

New Testament references also indicate that God desires to fellowship with us. First Corinthians 1:9 tells us that God has called us into fellowship with Jesus. Among other things, that means we share in His sufferings (Philippians 3:10). John calls believers to have fellowship with the disciples, which he then says leads to fellowship with the Father and the Son (1 John 1:3, 6–7). Fellowship indicates unity, and we see that concept illustrated in the figures of the vine and the branches (John 15:1–5) and of the head and the body (1 Corinthians 12:12, Colossians 1:18). These verses describe a specific communion between Jesus and believers as well as our communion with the Father.

Other verses show that fellowship among believers is beautiful and desirable as we see in David and Jonathan, in brothers dwelling together in unity in Psalm 133, and in the closeness shared by Paul and the elders at Ephesus. Even the lament of the psalmist in Psalm 55:12–14 indicates that companionship and friendship is sweet fellowship, and fellowship broken through the insult of a close friend brings anguish that can hardly be endured.

God created us to be in relationship with Him and one another. That relationship should be characterized by the kind of love and fellowship that exists within the Godhead. Our social nature, then, is an expression of the communication and fellowship within the Trinity. The characteristics and work of each human being are to find their expression in the context of shared experience with God and humankind. The educational process must be designed to foster the development of this shared experience or fellowship. Individual effort and achievement, or even one's individual relationship to God, should not crowd out the communal and relational dimension of reflecting God's image.

Loving

Love is such a pervasive characteristic of God that the apostle John actually says that "God is love" (1 John 4:8, 16). Paul tells us that God has demonstrated His love for us through Christ's death while we were yet sinners (Romans 5:8) and that He has poured His love into our hearts by giving us the Holy Spirit (Romans 5:5). As a result, we are commanded to walk in love (Ephesians 5:2, NKJV) and are repeatedly exhorted to "love one another" (John 13:34–35, 15:12; 1 John 4:7, 11, 21; 2 John 5). God's love for us is demonstrated in numerous ways, but at least three ways are significant for us in examining how our human nature should demonstrate God's image. Let's examine them one by one.

God exhibits His love for sinful, fallen human beings through *offering forgiveness*. While forgiveness is a major theme of the New Testament, it certainly is found in the Old Testament as well. Moses asks the Lord, "In accordance with your great love, forgive the sin of these people, just as you have pardoned them from the time they left Egypt until now" (Numbers 14:19). God tells Jeremiah that He will "forgive their wickedness and ... remember their sins no more" (Jeremiah 31:34). The psalmist recognizes that with God there is forgiveness (Psalm 130:4), and Nehemiah declares that God is a forgiving God (Nehemiah 9:17). Consequently, we are called to forgive as we are forgiven (Matthew 6:14–15, 18:21–22, 35; Luke 6:37). In fact, these passages make a clear connection between forgiving others and receiving God's forgiveness. We whom God has forgiven have an obligation to forgive others. If we do not do so, we demonstrate that we have never received God's forgiveness. It seems clear that this is one of the major ways of demonstrating God's character to our fellow human beings, and if we fail to demonstrate it, the consequences are severe. Forgiveness is a huge issue in the lives of students who come from such broken circumstances, and we cannot overlook that.

A second way that God demonstrates His love for us is by *doing what is just and good*. Joseph saw that even what human beings sometimes intend for evil, God turns into good (Genesis 50:20). Psalm 145:9 tells us, "The Lord is good to all," and Psalm 84:11 indicates that God does not withhold any good thing from us. Deuteronomy 32:4 states, "His works are perfect ... his ways are just," and He "does no wrong," in spite of the fact that the succeeding verse indicates that His people have acted corruptly toward Him and are a warped and crooked generation. Two ideas show that we are expected to follow God's footsteps in doing good. We are commended by God when we do good acts (Hezekiah in 2 Chronicles 31:20), and we are commanded to do what is good. We should "do good to all people" (Galatians 6:10), and we should seek the good of others over our own good (1 Corinthians 10:24). Likewise, Proverbs 1:3 exhorts us to acquire wisdom for "doing what is right and just and fair"; Micah 6:8 tells us that God requires us "to act justly." We clearly exhibit love to our fellow human beings by acting in these ways and thus again demonstrate God's character. What happens when we as teachers "do good" to our students and when they "do good" to others?

A third way in which God shows His love for us, and perhaps the major way, is through *sacrificing Himself* (in Jesus) for others (John 3:16; 1 John 3:16, 4:9–10; Romans 5:8, 8:32; Philippians 2:5–8). Isaiah predicted the sacrifice (chapter 53), and the entire Old Testament sacrificial system was a shadow of what was to come in the sacrifice of Jesus. Sacrifice, a giving of self for the benefit of others, is then to become a way of life for us. Such teaching is made clear in Jesus' challenges to turn the other cheek, to give the cloak as well as the tunic, to go the extra mile, and to love our enemies (Matthew 5:38–44). Paul urged the Philippians to consider others better than themselves, looking to the interests of others rather than their own. Jesus did not cling to His equality with God but humbled Himself (Philippians 2:6–8). We are indeed called to do the same.

Undoubtedly, God has demonstrated His love toward us in many more ways, and we should mirror that characteristic in many more ways as well. But the three ways mentioned above—forgiving, doing what is good, and sacrificing oneself— are particular themes in the Scriptures that call our students to live out God's image through love. They may be far from it in their current state, but still, loving is a part of who God made them to be.

Merciful

To receive mercy is to *not* receive what is deserved. God's mercy is plainly evident when we think of what we were when He demonstrated His love toward us. It is clear that no one was righteous or was seeking God (Psalms 14:1–3, 53:1–3; Ecclesiastes 7:20; Romans 3:9–18). The Scriptures portray all human beings as not seeking or thinking they need God because they believe they are self-sufficient and righteous in themselves—the ultimate affront against God. Titus 3:3–5 describes us as "foolish, disobedient, deceived and enslaved by all kinds of passions and pleasures," living in malice and envy and hating one another. Such results should be expected when we see ourselves as sufficient and independent of God. But it was in this miserably offensive condition that God chose to save us, *because of His mercy.*

God declares Himself to be merciful (Jeremiah 3:12), as do the many writers of the Scriptures. Moses tells God's people that the Lord their "God is a merciful God" (Deuteronomy 4:31). Samuel declares that God's mercy is great (2 Samuel 24:14). Daniel says, "The Lord our God is merciful" (9:9). The psalmist calls Him merciful (Psalm 78:38). And as God's people confess their sins under Ezra's preaching, they acknowledge that God is gracious and merciful in not putting an end to their arrogant and stiff-necked forefathers (Nehemiah 9:31).

That our students should likewise be merciful if they are to reflect God's image in dealing with others can be asserted without question. God again gives us specific instruction in His Word to that effect. Jesus claims that the merciful are blessed (Matthew 5:7) and exhorts His followers to be merciful as their Father is merciful (Luke 6:36). The parable of the unmerciful servant (Matthew 18:21–35) is a sobering illustration of what awaits those who have received mercy but are then unwilling to extend it to others. God declares that He desires mercy rather than sacrifice from us (Hosea 6:6; Micah 6:6–8; Matthew 9:13, 12:7), indicating its importance to Him. Jude 22 urges us to "be merciful to those who doubt," and James says that "mercy triumphs over judgment" (2:13). Demonstrating mercy to others is certainly one means (though not the only one) of demonstrating love. If our educational process does not teach students to be merciful, they will not learn to love—bringing dishonor to God by failing to reveal His character in tangible ways.

Dependent

The final attribute we will discuss indicates a great chasm between God and human beings. In fact, the characteristic in humans is not seen simply as a distorted version of the characteristic in God; rather, it is the complete opposite. It is the total distinction between the *Creator* and the *created*.

God "is not served by human hands, as if he needed anything, because he himself gives all men life and breath and everything else" (Acts 17:25). "For from him and through him and to him are all things" (Romans 11:36). He is truly the independent, self-sufficient Creator of all that is. We, on the other hand, as the created beings, are totally dependent on the Creator for everything. "In Him, we live and move and exist" (Acts 17:28, NASB). As Psalm 36:9 tells us, our knowledge is dependent on Him: "In your light we see light." Our physical sustenance is in Him (Matthew 6:25–33).

Only God can satisfy the deepest longings of our students' souls (Psalm 62:1, 5), and only He can meet our need to be loved and accepted. God created us to be in fellowship with Him and to be loved by Him. Obedience maintains the relationship of love, security, and acceptance, but disobedience brings separation and fear. Is this not also our experience with our students, and theirs with one another?

Of course, we are dependent not only on God but also on our fellow human beings. "The body is a unit, though it is made up of many parts; and though all its parts are many, they form one body" (1 Corinthians 12:12). "We are all members of one body" (Ephesians 4:25); in fact, "we are members of his body" (Ephesians 5:30). Parts of a body are dependent on one another, and so are human beings. The malfunction of one part affects all the other parts, as does each part's successful functioning. The bad action of one student affects the whole class.

Our students delude themselves in thinking that they can be independent, or even that they should be. They may become dependent on the wrong people, the wrong gods, or the wrong ideas, but they are certainly dependent creatures. As teachers we can foster a proper sense of dependence or ignore it. The latter will have dire consequences.

A Summary of Key Points

The list of attributes discussed thus far is not meant to be all-inclusive; rather, it is meant to identify the attributes that cannot be ignored in the educational process. Human beings, made in the image of God, must be treated as such during the teaching and learning process. For quick reference, the following is a composite list of attributes that should make a significant impact on our teaching when we consider learners as image bearers:

- *Active and purposeful.* Humans act to create ideas and things, making sense of things in relation to themselves, in an effort to exercise some manner of control over the world around them.
- *Rational.* We seek to perceive and understand, to conceptualize, to form and evaluate, and to relate intellectually to what is around us.
- *Creative.* We form ideas and make things out of what God has created, placing value judgments on what we have created.
- *Moral.* We act in relation to standards of right and wrong, and our actions tend to bring about justice or injustice.
- *Free and responsible.* We make choices and judgments according to our purposes, acting freely within the boundaries and limits of our created nature. We are also accountable for our choices and behavior, not simply victims of the environment and circumstances.
- *Faithful.* We are creatures of faith, believing something to be true and acting on it. We are committed either to the one true God or some substitute (thing or idea) created by human beings. We worship something.
- *God's stewards.* As we think, create, and act in purposeful ways, we exercise control over what is around us, creating a culture and acting as God's stewards of the creation.
- *Social.* Relationship is at the heart of our existence. We are meant to live in fellowship with God and others, sharing meaningful experiences.
- *Loving.* We were created to love and be loved. We are called to demonstrate that characteristic by forgiving others, doing what is best for them, and sacrificing ourselves for them.

- *Merciful.* As part of our love for others, we are called on to extend mercy to others as we have received God's mercy.
- *Dependent.* We are created and totally dependent on the Creator for our being and continued existence. We also are dependent on fellow human beings and the environment around us.

We cannot stop with just the created attributes, however. As we have already seen, the fall drastically affected all of creation, especially human beings. In the next chapter, we will consider just what the entrance of sin brought to humanity.

Now What?

As you consider your identified students, which image-bearing characteristics seem to be most evident in them, even if displayed in destructive ways? How could you focus on and encourage those characteristics in them?

9 The Image Marred

Clearly, we do not always live out God's image in ways that please Him. In fact, apart from God's intervention, all the acts that we do as His image bearers are distorted, turned away from their proper purpose. This would be obvious in thinking about many of the children who come to our classes—their sin is the most apparent thing about them. And as significant as it is for us to understand how to deal with learners as God's image bearers, we must be aware of the effects of sin on that image and on our actions. We ignore these effects at our own peril and that of our students.

Our examination of the nature of human beings as learners must, then, include a look at the effects of sin. Sin entered the world as Adam and Eve chose to disobey God (Genesis 3:1–7). Since that time, humans have been conceived and born in a state of sinfulness (Psalm 51:5, Romans 5:12, Ephesians 2:3). No one escapes the consequence of Adam's sin, but the fact that we are born in a state of sinfulness is not all we need to know. We need to see the practical implications of that fact before it can have an impact on us.

Perversion and Pollution, Not Elimination

We recognize that sin in any category of life involves the denial of reality as God has created and revealed it. Because we cannot live apart from some system of truth, we have no alternative but to restructure reality according to our own design. In so doing, we attempt in perverted ways to fulfill our role of bearing God's image and managing the creation. The results are polluted air and water, perverted structures of government and marriage, and destructive behaviors in classrooms. All that we do to fulfill what we are called to be is distorted and headed in the wrong direction, but it does not disappear (Frey et al. 1983).

The effect of sin, then, is to pervert rather than destroy. God hates our perversion of His structures such as marriage and government, not the structures themselves. After all, He created those structures. His judgment and wrath is on the abuse of them. The structure of marriage, for instance, has been badly distorted, but we do not see God doing away with the idea or institution of marriage.

A similar situation exists concerning the effects of the fall on human beings. We did not become nonpersons or cease to bear the image of God as a result of the fall—a fact that we as teachers must remember as we deal with our students. We did not lose our being or our task in life, nor did they; rather, we both have become morally perverted and totally misdirected. Our lives are lived out in a state of personal disunity, but they are still human lives (Jaarsma 1961). Our unrighteousness has had devastating effects, but the fact that we are still human requires that we be treated as such.

Idolatry

After the fall, human beings became transient (Cain for example), wandering from idol to idol, from delusion to delusion. We are no longer God-centered, God-serving, God-enjoying, or God-obeying, but rather we are self-centered, self-serving, self-enjoying, and self-obeying (DeJong 1977). We are still creatures of faith, but not faith in the one true God. Because we are dependent, we still need security. But now, because of sin our search for security is turned away from God, the only true source of security. Unable to adequately provide such security for ourselves, our search may become frenetic, bizarre, or destructive, always ending in some type of idolatry. This would be very true of many of the students we encounter on a daily basis, would it not?

It is important to realize that the nature of idolatry is an exchange—something we do instead of serving God (Walsh and Middleton 1984). It may take many forms, but essentially, we first declare our independence from God and His rightful kingship, and then we substitute something else (the perversion) to worship and serve. As we remove God from the scene, we remove His standards for order and justice. This is the reason lawlessness and injustice so often follow idolatry. Romans 1:23 and 25 describe the perverted, idolatrous exchange, and verses 26 through 32 tell of the awful results.

As Satan tempted Adam to make this declaration of independence, what followed was a clashing of two kingdoms—light (God's) and darkness (Satan's). We were created for light, but we find ourselves living in darkness. The light-giving communion with the Creator was cut off, and life itself has become broken rather than whole, dark rather than light. Interpersonal and societal breakdowns have occurred as our declaration of independence and the substituted idols have proved to be illusory. Genuine security cannot be found in the kingdom of darkness, though our students seek it there all the time.

Since the earth was also cursed as a result of this declaration, we experience earth as an enemy (Genesis 3:17–19). (Serving idols always leads to this experience because they are enemies.) We are driven to conquer the earth instead of to care for it, and our rule is as disobedient as our declaration was. And while God still calls our students to an obedient response in caring for the creation, Satan bids them to pledge allegiance to the renegade kingdom and to deny their true calling. Apart from God's intervention, that is exactly what they will do because it is all they are capable of doing (Walsh and Middleton 1984). Our "culture creating" is as perverted as our personal behavior.

Estrangement

In addition to experiencing the creation as an enemy, human beings are affected very deeply by the fall in terms of personal relationships—with God, others, and ourselves. Brokenness is felt more deeply here than in any other realm of life. When we suppress the truth of God (Romans 1:18), refuse to acknowledge Him (1:20), profess to be wise (1:22), and worship the creature rather than the Creator (1:25), the results in terms of relationships are disastrous.

Estrangement from God. The first estrangement (or separation) from God occurred in the garden when after their sin Adam and Eve became afraid of God. Their reaction was to hide (Genesis 3:8–10). God took the next step in this estrangement and cast them out of the garden (Genesis 3:22–24). Cain declared his independence by deciding what type of offering was acceptable to God. Soon after, he murdered his brother Abel. God placed a curse on Cain (Genesis 4:11) and destined him to be a fugitive (separation again).

Isaiah pronounces a woe on him who quarrels with his Maker (45:9), and anyone who quarrels knows the separation that either causes or results from a quarrel. Quarreling with God is a serious offense. It breaks fellowship because it is a rejection of God's truth, and that rejection is the heart of sin.

Estrangement from others. If quarreling with God is connected to our separation from Him, quarreling with our fellow human beings is evidence of our separation from them as well (Proverbs 17:19). Quarreling with others seems to be the natural result of turning to our own desires (James 4:1–2), and the jealousy among us likewise reveals a commitment to be more concerned with ourselves and our things than with others (1 Corinthians 3:3). The insistence on being right in a discussion (another form of an unrighteous concern for self rather than others) often leads to quarreling and resentment (2 Timothy 2:23–24). The servant of the Lord is instructed to avoid such behavior and to be kind to everyone. A quarrelsome person kindles strife with others instead of bringing healing (Proverbs 26:21), a sure sign of separation rather than unity.

This estrangement from others is a direct result of separation from God. Since our students have denied God and replaced His truth with that of their own making and have focused on providing for their own security in their own way, they have developed all manner of strife and destruction in their relationships with others, all who suffer from the same malady. The description of this destruction provided in Romans 1:28–31 is frightening—"every kind of wickedness, evil, greed … envy, murder, strife, deceit, malice," gossip, slander, insolence, arrogance, boastfulness, disobedience, senselessness, faithlessness, heartlessness, and ruthlessness—each an offense against human beings as well as God. Truly, in our fallen state we are separated from one another.

Estrangement from self. A third and equally serious estrangement may be a bit more difficult to understand, and it is sometimes more difficult to deal with. We are not only separated from God and others, but we are separated from our true selves as well. Most of us deny this, as somehow, we all like to think that we personally have things together. We think that whatever trouble may exist in relationships with others must be their fault, whether we are teachers or students. Whether or not we admit that our experience tells us differently, the Scriptures make it clear that we suffer from "internal" conflict and we are attuned not to what God created us to be but to the sin within us.

Romans 7:15–24 is an excellent description of this conflict, even in the life of a believer. Paul realizes what is right and good, and even desires to do it, yet he finds himself doing otherwise because of the sin that is in him. Likewise, David, the man after God's own heart, wrestled with his sin. He said it troubled him (Psalm 38:18), and he knew his soul could find "rest in God alone" (Psalm 62:1, 5). Thus, even though believers are secure and we have an identity that rests in Christ, we still live in a state of internal conflict and we are unable to completely be what we were created to be, because of our sin. The image is indeed marred, and it will be raised as perfect and complete only at the resurrection day.

Those who reject God (unbelievers) also reject what they were created to be. Instead of being free to serve God and reflect His image righteously, they become slaves to their sin (John 8:34, Romans 6:16). In other words, the "cords of his sin hold him fast" (Proverbs 5:22), and "a man is a slave to whatever has mastered him" (2 Peter 2:19). So while believers live in a battlefield between God and Satan, unbelievers live in the only state possible for them—enslaved to the sin of a fallen, idol-worshiping self, not able or willing to admit that they were created to worship and serve God but having rejected Him instead. They still bear the image of God, but their every effort is spent trying to be self-sufficient and acceptable on their own merit. They are still trying to *be* God rather than to *be like* God, and therefore they are committed to believing and acting on a lie—a lie about God, reality, and themselves. As they deny the truth about God, they are cut off from God. Likewise, as they deny the truth about themselves, they are cut off from their true selves. For how many of our students would this be true?

Seeking Security

Human beings were created to be secure, but since we have cut ourselves off from the true source of security, we naturally seek it elsewhere. We have already seen that we were created and we are therefore dependent, and thus our true security must be found outside ourselves. As mentioned in our discussion of idolatry, we may commit ourselves to any kind of false god—material thing or idea—in order to find some security. However, because the nature of our sin is to preempt God, to try to be God, we also often seek security in ourselves. As mentioned in chapter 1, our students are often desperate to find security somewhere.

Western humanism has long been especially prominent in promoting the view that we can be secure only in ourselves. There is no divine purpose for human life; humans are responsible for what they will become. No deity will save them; they must save themselves. Moral values are derived from human experience, and ethics stem from human need and interest.

With this emphasis on finding one's identity and security from within oneself, students often seek it through their personal attributes or performance. Those who are beautiful, smart, or athletic can be someone (Dobson 1974). Those who are successful in making money and friends, acquiring goods or awards, or advancing in a career can be secure (Campolo 1980). Accomplishment brings recognition and an accompanying sense of being accepted—a prerequisite to security.

On the other hand, those who are not beautiful or smart or not successful in hardly anything feel the rejection that failure brings. They are left with a sense of little or no worth. Those who cannot perform and succeed are basically nobodies. Those who are overweight or unattractive are not worth much. Those who have no sense of value or worth at home, who are told they will amount to nothing, or who are simply never engaged as persons at home, will almost always seek to find their identity in destructive ways. And, they walk into your classrooms in such a state.

Self-Referenced

Of necessity, we all view life from our own perspective. As our students grow in life, they form a view of reality that is uniquely their own. As events unfold, they relate them to themselves and their beliefs, for there is no other meaningful way to interact with what is happening around them. The self must serve as a reference point since they cannot live outside themselves. This is not a problem for a self that is in a proper relationship with the Creator, but it becomes a problem for a self living under the fall.

While it is impossible for our students to view life apart from who they are, using the self as the final reference point creates considerable difficulty. Just as they seek security in themselves, they also measure all others through their own perspective. When they become their own final authority, they judge the behavior, values, beliefs, and thoughts of all others against the standards they have set. The more insecure they are, the more authoritative their own perspective may become. There is little room to accommodate differing perspectives unless, of course, their perspective is that all perspectives are acceptable. (Such relativity regarding truth can also make one feel quite secure since no one can ever be wrong.) In either case, they decide just what will be accepted and will fit their own perspective on the way things should be.

Needless to say, either approach to truth is troublesome. The rigid "I am right" attitude leads to conflict and separation from others. People with such an attitude fail to realize that either they are blinded to truth through unbelief or they see things dimly at best (1 Corinthians 13:12, NKJV). This approach also leaves one with little room to grow, as there is little or no opportunity to assimilate new ideas or experiences. The challenge of learning becomes a threat to their personal security.

Of course, just the opposite is true. Being so closed-minded is dangerous, for not only does it cut one off from others and reduce the opportunity to grow, it also once again sets us human beings up to be God. Those who are always right have no need for God, even when they claim that all their knowledge of the truth came from God. Such a claim may in fact be the most dangerous position of all because it puts the person above the possibility of being wrong. Who can argue with those who claim God as their authority? While they claim that God is their authority and reference point, in reality they are using themselves as both.

The "accept all perspectives" approach is equally troublesome. Adherence to this perspective is sometimes as rigid as the previous one. A belief that no one approach to truth is better than another is simply unacceptable. Interestingly though, "there are no absolutes" becomes an absolute—a true contradiction within the system.

But even if our students' adherence to accepting all views is not so rigid, we find ourselves dealing with another dangerous situation. If no perspective is better than another, what happens when two personal perspectives clash? On what basis can one decide what is right and what to do? The "accept all" perspective, while meant to provide the opportunity for all to live in *unity*, actually leaves us all *separated*, living in our own private worlds and careful not to encroach upon the private world of another. No wonder students find themselves so alone and without fellowship! There is no common truth or purpose; they all have their own individual purposes, and they must pursue them on their own. They again find themselves cut off from others. To use the self as the final authority and reference point can only result in being alone.

Inability to Solve the Problem on Our Own

Sin brought judgment and wrath on both humankind and the creation (Genesis 3:14–19). While we did something to create the predicament, we can do nothing to correct it. In our rejection of God, we refuse to believe we are helpless in solving our predicament, and we live as if we can fix it, though that is simply another denial of the truth. Like a turtle on its back, we are unable to right ourselves. Because of our created nature, we cannot change a decree of the Creator. Consequently, the solution to our problem of sin cannot come from within us. It must come from the Creator alone.

Paul recognized that he could not have confidence in his own self and doings. He said that if any man had reason to believe that his own person and accomplishments would earn him the favor of God, he did. Yet he considered those things to be "rubbish" (Philippians 3:4–9). The reconciliation of humankind to God and creation can be accomplished only through God's grace, not human effort (Ephesians 2:8–9, 2 Timothy 1:9, Titus 3:5). The pursuit of the solution on any basis other than faith is doomed to failure (Romans 9:30–32).

Even the temporal blessings we receive cannot be attributed simply to our own righteousness (Deuteronomy 9:4–6). In fact, our righteous acts are compared to filthy rags (Isaiah 64:6). While righteous obedience to God does carry the promise of blessing, obedience is not possible apart from an act of God to change our heart and direction of life. Thus any righteous act we do perform that pleases God cannot ultimately be attributed to ourselves; it is possible only through our union with Christ. Though we created the problem, we cannot solve it by ourselves.

Thus, just as Jesus "entered into" the lives of His broken people to reveal the nature of God toward them, as Jesus' representatives to our students so must we.

The Image Marred: A Summary

As we have looked at humankind after the fall, we have seen several characteristics that are important in understanding just how we as Christians should teach. Human beings in our fallen state are the following:

- *Perverted, not eliminated.* All the created attributes of humankind were distorted and misdirected at the fall. They did not disappear and make us something other than human. We still bear the image of God, though that image is perverted in every dimension.

- *Idolatrous.* We exchanged the truth of God for a lie, but we continue to be creatures of faith, believing in and acting on whatever we choose to believe is true.

- *Estranged.* Because of our sin, we are separated from God, others, and ourselves, not adequately knowing any of the three or how to respond appropriately.

- *Seeking security.* Cut off from the true source of security, we seek it not only in the idols we create but also in ourselves and our performance.

- *Self-referenced.* Having denied God as the authority and reference point for all of life, we use ourselves for both, usurping God's place.

- *Unable to solve the problem ourselves.* We cannot undo the effects of the fall and remove ourselves from God's judgment through our own efforts. It takes an act of God to bring healing and the possibility of righteousness.

Now What?

How do you see your chosen students as estranged from God, others, and self? How do they reveal their search for security?

10 No Safe Place to Seek Answers

As we found in chapter 1, students are always faced with the three big questions: "Who am I?" "Will I be OK?" and "What am I to be about in this world?" just as teachers are. One of their great problems is that they have no safe place in which they can search for the answers. Family, friends, school, church—all want to tell them who they are to be, how to behave in order to be accepted and secure, and to do what is expected of them, mostly to make life more convenient for the one who is doing the telling. There is little, if any, grace given to them in the process, and little thought is given by any of these groups to what it means for them to be created in the image of God. Teachers are often more concerned about teaching students information than in helping them answer the big three questions.

A Safe Place Is a Place of Grace

Why do I say that? Because our fallen nature still plagues (though does not *define*) us, things will constantly go wrong. If, every time something goes wrong, the just desert is dished out, life is driven by fear. We are never safe if the basic rule of life is "We get what we deserve." Yet how much of the world, how much of life in school, and how much of life lived in all the contexts mentioned above follows exactly that rule?

That, however, is not the way grace operates. The nature of grace is to receive favor when we deserve judgment. Grace is undeserved favor. In a place of grace, there need be no fear, because grace is a demonstration of the love of God and love is what casts out fear (1 John 4:18).

A lack of grace forces students to be self-protective, defensive, sometimes overly resistant, and sometimes overly compliant. The name of the game is to figure out what the authority wants and then to give it; or if students fail at that enough times, they don't care what the authority wants, and they protect themselves by disengaging or rebelling.

However, if students know they will be treated with dignity—even when being disciplined—that they are going to be heard, and that a teacher cares more about students than an ordered, high-achieving classroom, students may feel very differently. They will feel that they are being treated like the image bearers they are.

If instead of constantly receiving the just desert for wrongdoing, students receive another chance; if a teacher seems to want to enter students' pain or suffering or problem that may have prompted the failure or bad behavior; if students are not treated as fools when they don't know something they should, but a teacher tries to bring something good out of what they have said or written or tries to help them find the right answer; if a teacher trusts students with responsibility even when they have not necessarily earned it—well, then they are in a safe place, a place of grace.

A Safe Place Is a Place of Understanding

When we are searching desperately for a sense of who we are and to know that who we are is of some value, what difference does it make when we sense that someone "gets" us? What difference does it make when we sense someone really "gets" what is going on with us, especially when that may not be very attractive? What difference does it make to us that Jesus was God "incarnate?" If we truly accept that He came to experience all the things we experience and that He knows and identifies completely with all our sufferings and losses and wounds, what does that do for us? (Our problem often is that we can give lip service to that idea, but we have little actual "experience" with it because we have never allowed our relationship to become that intimate.)

Not feeling understood is one of the loneliest experiences of life. Not being understood means not being received. It causes us to question if we have any value. When students are not understood and wonder if they have any value, what do we expect of them? Do we think they will be calm, focused, obedient, and interested in multiplying fractions or writing essays or studying ancient history?

When we don't understand them, it is hard to connect to them in terms of what matters to them, and if things don't matter to them it is a sure thing that they will not put much energy into them. And if we try to force them to, what does that do to their sense of being understood and received? If the things that matter to them don't matter to us, then they themselves don't matter to us. Who wants to work hard and follow someone who sends out a message that a person doesn't matter?

In a Safe Place We Feel Protected

My kindergarten and first-grade teacher (the same woman) colored my view of school and life in a big way. I was already a fearful little boy, and she helped drive that fear deep into my being. Life in her classroom was not safe.

One day a crayon rolled off my desk, and she made me stay after school because I was being too noisy. I became so fearful of displeasing her that each morning I came to school I had to run to the boys' room because I was sure I was going to vomit. Though not all my teachers were this extreme, I can remember several whose basic mode of operation was to instill fear into us so that we would learn and do what was right. I learned, and I was driven by, the lesson of fear for decades.

There were occasional teachers who were different though. It seemed as if they actually liked us, enjoyed us, and cared for us. They were friendly to us. They did not fight with us, resist us, or have a need for ironfisted control. If things were not going well, we knew they were on our side.

One teacher in particular never even had to raise his voice in class. We respected him, trusted him, and followed his lead. A fellow student once fell asleep in class, and he did not wake up when the bell rang to dismiss us. The rest of us got up to leave, saw what had happened, and snickered, thinking, "Oh boy, is he in for trouble." The teacher just smiled gently, walked over and touched the boy's shoulder, and said it was time to leave. No anger, no chiding, no ridiculing—just a smile and a touch of grace, in a place that was safe.

This teacher taught all my high school mathematics classes and my physics class. I wonder if that had anything to do with the fact that I became a math and physics teacher myself. Even more important, I know how much his example has influenced the way I have dealt with my own students, even the way I have viewed what school is and what it should be about. And though I did not fully understand it at the time, I eventually came to know that what made this man different is that he *walked* with God. Because he walked with God, he could make the classroom a safe place instead of one where he had to threaten us all to keep us in line.

Oh, I knew from his words and example that he was a Christian (though I had very little real understanding of what that meant at the time), but many of us claimed to be the same. I was a good churchgoing boy, and I sometimes thought that maybe he took his Christianity a bit too seriously. Only later, once I surrendered my own life to Jesus, did I begin to get the picture of what made this man so different. He was a friend of God, and it could not help but ooze out of his being into the way he loved us, his students.

He never outwardly tried to make a disciple of me. It just happened—because of who he was and how much time I spent around him in the classroom, at ball games, in extracurricular activities, and even at his son's birthday parties. His life flowed into me, and I could not escape it. I do not ever remember being afraid in his presence. My life was changed because of a relationship with this man who walked with God.

In a Safe Place We Are Encouraged to Fly

As a high school mathematics teacher, I taught the geometry course. Geometry is often taught with an emphasis on generating "proofs." Many students wonder what the point is. Some people love geometry, and others hate it. In either case, seldom are students given much of an opportunity to be creative. Rather, logical deductive thinking is required, and students have to be very analytical.

One of the more interesting parts of geometry has to do with shapes—geometric figures can be rather fascinating. One particular year I remember that I had a class of students with quite a variety of levels of understanding, skill, and interest in geometry. I expect many of them would tell you (decades later!) that the most (maybe only!) memorable and significant portion of the class was the two weeks that we set aside for them to create a geometric design of their own choosing.

The task appeared somewhat daunting to some at the beginning; others dove in like ducks into water. They also were not used to creativity being part of their academic work—especially in mathematics classes. It could have felt very unsafe, and they could have become paralyzed. But they did not. Instead, they created some of the most unbelievable two- and three-dimensional shapes and designs that I had ever seen.

One boy had a ten-faced three-dimensional figure that he came up with a name for, and I simply looked at it in awe. Years later I saw his mother, and she told me he had kept it for display well into his professional career as an engineer. Others were more modest, but nearly all represented a creation that was well beyond what they imagined themselves able to do. They flew higher than they thought they could, and I am convinced that a major part of the reason they could do so was because they knew it was safe to try. Our personal relationship, the grading procedures I had instituted for the course, the encouragement they received along the way, the respect and trust I gave them to produce their own things—all these made that experience and that classroom a safe place.

In a Safe Place Our Sense of Awe and Wonder Is Expanded

To experience awe and wonder is to enter a world of uncertainty, a world of mystery, a world where all is not reduced to categories and subjected to analysis. It is a world where we do not have control over anything. It just *is*, and we *are*, and the connection between the two cannot be articulated well in words.

If we were to try to describe a sunset only scientifically, think what a minimizing of the experience we would have to do.

If we were to try to grammatically analyze a love poem, think what injustice to love we would be doing.

If mathematical formulas were used only to solve practical problems, think what a puny appreciation for mathematics that would be.

If history were a mere chronology of events, with no consideration of what was going on in the hearts and lives of those who made the history, how reductionistic and inhuman would that be?

If school is a place where students are rewarded for finding the right answers and punished for not finding them, it is a place of *fear*. One cannot wonder, think out of the box, creatively seek solutions to practical problems, or risk being wrong in any way. It is not safe to be fully human, only robotic. For humans were created to respond to God and His creation in awe. And His thoughts are so high above ours that we can only wonder …

In a safe place we can get out of the box, explore, come up with conclusions that no one else will make, and if we make mistakes we are not punished. Rather, we are affirmed for trying, for stretching ourselves, and we are encouraged to rethink and try again.

Safe Places Are Created Through Relationships

Ever since the fall of Adam and Eve, broken relationships result in fear, shame, and guilt. Where broken relationships prevail, there is no safety. Nor is there much chance of growth or moving forward in life. A relationship with a teacher that enables broken students to know that they are loved and accepted where they are, that tells them they are of great value even in their brokenness, and that treats them like image bearers of God provides the safe place necessary for them to learn and grow.

As teachers it is our desire to change lives, and lives are seldom changed through verbal or written instruction. *Lives are changed through relationship and experience.* Jesus came to restore our relationship to God, and the experience He gave to those who would accept it was grace. When we as teachers seek to create relationships with students that reflect our own relationship with Jesus, we cannot do it except out of a framework of grace.

A place of grace is a safe place, and when that grace is demonstrated by a teacher who deals with broken students as Jesus deals with us, lives can change. Learning can take a child somewhere. To explore, to develop a new pattern of behavior (leave a bad one and try a new one), to be what students were created by God to be, to exchange a faulty set of values for a better one—all these things require a safe place. And a safe place is created by teachers who seek to have relationships with students that come from their own relationship with Jesus.

Now What?

What could you do to make your classroom, and yourself, a safe place for your students to seek answers to the three big questions they ask: "Who am I?" "Will I be OK?" and "What am I to be about?"

Part 4

When Grace Pervades the Classroom

11 | Curriculum Choices

Many factors affect the choices we make in our curriculum. State requirements are a big factor, and what follows is not meant to diminish those requirements in the least. It is, however, meant to challenge us to think about how our Christian faith convictions should also influence choices we make in the curriculum. So let's examine a classroom where those convictions would affect our choices.

What Biblical Ideas Should Affect the Way We Structure the Curriculum?

The first act of grace toward students comes in our treating them as image bearers of God. We remind ourselves that students were created to be as follows:

- Active and purposeful
- Rational
- Creative
- Moral
- Free and responsible
- Faithful

- Stewards
- Social
- Loving
- Merciful
- Dependent

Though this image is marred by the fall, nevertheless it is still the most fundamental nature of a student. Therefore, choices we make in the curriculum must reflect that, and as they do, those choices become a part of the process and atmosphere of grace that must be prevalent in our classrooms and schools.

Curriculum is defined in many different ways. I wish to go beyond the idea that it is merely the "subjects" offered in the school and to suggest that we look at curriculum as those planned learning experiences over which the teachers have some influence. Granted, much learning occurs outside the classroom, and it may have virtually no input from the teacher, but that learning is very hard to get a grip on. Much learning may come through serendipity as well, but that, too, is quite beyond our control.

We also need to realize that merely planning the learning experiences does not ensure that students will learn what we want them to. Nevertheless, if we think we should influence what students learn at all, we must plan learning experiences to take them from one place in life to another. That plan, in its overall vision and structure, is what I would call curriculum design.

Integration. While human beings encounter and apprehend ideas and events as individual and unique, it is also true that they think and act to bring these diverse experiences into some kind of coherent whole. There is always an attempt to bring some unity to the diversity. That would suggest that teachers should make an obvious attempt to connect units of study and even other school subjects. Teachers who believe knowledge should be integrated also affirm the diversity of subjects, however, and they do not blur the distinctions between mathematics and social studies. However, in several ways the teachers seek to make connections between subject areas so that students experience knowledge not only in its diversity but also in its unity.

In most parts of the curriculum, the teachers will find it necessary to teach the various disciplines as essentially separate subjects. When this is the case, if teachers of the different subjects plan their activities to occur in support of (or connected with) the activities of other teachers who are teaching the same students, that would be a good thing. They plan units of study and exploration of topics that allow for connections to be made in the students' minds, and they work hard to make that happen through their common planning. This recognizes a part of what God created them to be as rational, creative stewards.

At other times, the teachers might plan for integrated teaching units, in which subjects are related to one another in a variety of ways. An issue such as poverty and wealth could be the core of the study, and information and research from various subject areas could be brought to bear on the issue. Students could be involved in studying mathematics, science, technology, economics, ethics, psychology, or other subjects in such a unit, and teachers who are experts in each of these areas could be involved in planning and executing the learning experiences.

When teachers pursue integration in a variety of ways, we never see them working in isolation, simply doing what they individually think is right. They seriously attempt to overcome fragmentation and disunity in the curriculum, and they are given the time and opportunity to plan and teach together in order to make it happen.

The responsibility of knowledge. Curriculum is not simply a matter of ideas and skills that are to be mastered intellectually. Skills and content are tied to one's responsibility to do something with what one knows. Units of study in all classes should include opportunities for students to respond to what they have learned. Their response may be through service projects, through teaching concepts and skills to others, but at least *doing something* with what they have learned. Mastery of the subject is not enough in itself, and the curriculum schedule includes time for students to live out what they have learned.

In fact, living out what they have learned is another part of the learning experience. The curriculum is designed so that students often reach conclusions in the process of learning rather than in listening as the teacher dispenses the correct conclusions and then expects the students to apply them. Consequently, the curriculum calls for the students to get outside the school building, to be aware of what is going on elsewhere in the world, and to be in contact with people outside their immediate sphere.

Sources of curriculum. This outside involvement represents another conviction about curriculum that is important—namely, that the issues of society are an important reason for our study and that they should influence what we study. So while the basic parameters of study stay generally the same each year in a given course, the particular questions dealt with and the specific units of study are modified from time to time depending on current events in the culture. Current events are not just something students do every Friday in social studies class. Particular events may alter the study for a given week or period of days, but current trends also determine what reading sources teachers select, what units of study they develop, and what research they ask their students to pursue.

But the issues of society do not dictate what happens in the curriculum; they are merely one important source. Another source is certainly the individual students. Because they bring a host of backgrounds and experiences to the learning task, they are asked to shape and design their individual pursuit of the questions when it is appropriate and possible. Projects allow for an individual twist depending on the students' motivations and gifts, and also their weaknesses. The questions that students are facing in life affect planning for the study as well, and the students have many opportunities to work with the teacher in developing the plan of study.

The individual character and procedures of the different academic disciplines also influence the curriculum, and teachers must appreciate the contributions that past study has made to the body of knowledge available to students today. Students should be taught not only the skills and content of a particular subject but also to understand the basic methods of inquiry used in that field. For instance, in history, the curriculum gradually expects students to do the work of historians, not simply to remember what other historians have said. In science, the curriculum includes the benefits and the limitations of the scientific method. Students study human behavior to discover why people behave the way they do. They also examine the problems that seriously limit our ability to draw definite conclusions about human behavior.

Finally, as Christian teachers we must consider the Bible as a source of curriculum. And while this is the arena where there seem to be many restrictions on public school teachers, we cannot simply dismiss the issue. We can consider how themes of Scripture inform the process of inquiry, how they shed light on and place limits on conclusions, how they help set parameters for the questions to be asked in the course of study, and how they are used to help the study of a particular subject lead students into a deeper awareness of who they are and how they are to relate to and care for the creation around them.

Biblical concepts and principles can be brought into study in this way without having to quote a passage or even verbally acknowledge where it came from. All teachers adhere to some kind of framework with such principles, and they are not necessarily required to state to students just what philosophy or worldview those principles came from. For instance, the principles of stewardship, caring for others, a stand against evil, the value of every human being, and so on are all biblical principles that can shape curriculum choices and that would be acceptable almost anywhere.

Focus on exploration and problem solving. In many schools the entire curriculum would be seen as an explanation of concepts or processes with the expectation that the students will understand the concepts and learn the skills that will then make them whole persons, contributing citizens, or whatever the school hopes they will become. Or, in an even more confining situation, the curriculum may be about meeting the state testing standards in order to continue to receive funding to operate. While both of these realities need to be accepted and faced, they do not have to ultimately define all curriculum choices.

As a demonstration of real life, students must sometimes explore questions that have not been asked in quite the same way before and that do not have a clear-cut answer. The curriculum could influence the school schedule enough so that it allows time for the students to pursue questions and problems in the community. If such were the case, we would seldom hear the argument that we cannot get involved in trying to solve tax problems for the poor because we will not have time to cover the social studies text. Rather, the teacher could choose social studies materials that will help the students figure out how to solve the tax problems for the poor.

Problems in the life of the school also influence the curriculum. When there is not enough equipment on the playground, students should work on solving that problem. When a fellow student has a learning problem, the students should get involved in helping. When it appears that some school policy may be unjust, students should deal with it and with those who are called on to enforce it.

Connection to life inside and outside the school. Curriculum should be meant to relate to life rather than to exist as an entity in itself. The questions that form the basis for the teaching units deal with the ways in which people experience life. The biblical themes used to undergird the teaching units and guide the exploration are chosen partly because of their relevance to life as students live it. Asking "What difference does this make?" is just as important as asking "What is this?"

Two Christian teachers in a public middle school have taken this idea of connecting to life outside the classroom, and they based their whole writing curriculum on it. The students in their school are primarily from a rural area where education is not necessarily the highest priority among families. Consequently, the state assessment scores of these children were historically not much to write home about. By giving the students something important to write about that connects to the outside world and making the students write essay after essay, the teachers helped the students in this eighth-grade class to rank number one in the annual state writing assessment two years in a row. Both teachers have won awards for their teaching. And the students' essays go out into the community to be read by people who are affected by the things they write about.

And What Does Grace Have to Do with Curriculum?

Curriculum design and grace. Grace does not design a curriculum. But it does influence the choices that we make about a curriculum. For instance, grace demands such a total response from students that we could never view the curriculum simply as the knowledge that they are to acquire in various subject areas or the skills they need to get along in life. What students learn must be translated into an ability to live out that grace in a fallen world that does not understand God's grace—another reason why students should be involved in solving real problems both inside and outside the classroom.

Grace demands gratitude, and gratitude is expressed through loving God and others. That expression cannot be learned or demonstrated by merely accumulating facts, discussing ideas, or reproducing facts and ideas on written assignments or tests. It must be demonstrated through contact with people who have real needs in real situations. Thus, the curriculum should be designed to engage students with what is going on in the world, not just to study it from textbooks. It gives them an opportunity to live out the reality of grace in dealing with broken life.

Believing that God deals graciously with students is also a factor in designing a curriculum that heavily emphasizes exploration and problem solving as ways of exercising the responsibility of knowledge. Were it not for the grace of God in leading the exploration and problem solving, and in dealing with misguided efforts and conclusions, we would not dare let the students explore and try to come to conclusions on their own. We could only tell them what to think and what to do. And we have seen how such an approach would deny students their being and their calling, and it would also deny our fallenness and our limitations as their teachers (who do all the "telling").

Attempting to help students understand the world of knowledge in an integrated manner requires a good deal of grace, for such an understanding in any complete sense is well beyond us. We are asking students to do something that is very difficult and that often leads to ambiguity. If we did not believe the grace of God to be active in such learning, we would have to believe the task to be impossible. But to deny integration and wholeness is to deny the way God made and sustains the world and the way He made us to experience it. It takes grace to let students make the attempt.

It also takes grace to expect students to deal with ideas and authors whose convictions and perspectives are contrary to biblical truth. Only the grace of God protects us from erroneous and evil input, and only His grace allows us to understand the kind of unbiblical thinking that drives the world. But we must remember that it is because of that grace that God sends us into the corrupt world to be salt and light and to demonstrate His grace in the process.

Our basic commitments regarding the purpose of education, the learner, the learning process, and the teacher also serve to shape the curriculum. Because a biblical view of educating should be holistic and integrated, we should not be surprised. And we shall see the impact of those commitments again and again as we examine the learning activities, the evaluation procedures, and classroom behavior. The ideas connect and support one another, just as they should.

Treating students as image bearers. We have already said that the first big act of grace to students is to treat them as the image bearers God made them to be. This too affects our approach to curriculum design. In particular, a design that engages the students in the curriculum as we have described treats them as image bearers. They are expected to think like God and then act like Him—actively, purposefully, and morally. Their attempts at understanding the diversity and unity of the universe also bring them closer to His perspective. And if they enter into situations inside and outside the school as from God's perspective, they will enter them as loving, merciful people.

The responsibility they bear to affect society with the things they know certainly recognizes their call to exercise dominion. The emphasis on exploration and problem solving allows them (and perhaps requires them) to be creative, rational, free, and responsible persons. And because the task is so large, it is very likely that they will always need to depend on one another and on God.

And what about the perversion and pollution of the image that resulted from the fall? Will that not distort the efforts of students and teachers alike so much that such an approach to curriculum will lead to little but frustration? Certainly the sinfulness of human beings leads to frustration as well as to error and distortion. But God does not deal with sinful people by controlling them so tightly that they do not make mistakes. Rather, it seems His love and grace are demonstrated most clearly right in the midst of messy situations with broken, fallen people. He seems to ask these fallen people to keep on thinking, working, and ministering, depending on the Spirit to guide them and on His grace to right the wrongs. What better reason could we have for a curriculum design that asks for input from the students, that encourages them to use what they know to help the broken world that needs them, and that connects them with life in an integrated biblical way?

The students' sinfulness is not a reason to keep them from activities in which learning could go wrong. On the contrary, freedom and responsibility to engage in such activity is one of the major things that the Lord has designed to make them aware of their dependence on Him. For when all goes right, who needs God? When teachers deal redemptively with things that go wrong, we see God at work showing a broken world who He is and how He operates. We shall soon see that dealing with fallen students in a fallen world requires the second big act of grace.

Now What?

What curriculum modifications or choices could you make that would reflect an effort to better treat your chosen students as image bearers and thus reveal a part of what grace is about?

12 Learning Activities and Assignments

Learning activities and assignments must be designed to work in concert with what we know about how people learn, and the way they learn is affected by the characteristics of the image of God in them. Once again, grace demands that we treat students as image bearers as we create the assignments we will give them. Let's see what that would look like.

What Is Consistent with Who They Are?

Remembering once more the characteristics of God that He has placed in our students, let's explore some possibilities of the types of things we might reasonably ask them to do.

Projects. Teachers who treat students as image bearers often ask students to work on large, long-term projects rather than small, discrete daily assignments. Such projects are likely to include discussion with human beings rather than merely research in books and other written materials. Primary sources are important. The teachers and the students discuss and decide on the most efficient and effective means of gathering necessary information, but gathering information to report and making pretty displays is seldom seen as the goal of the project.

Students and teachers work together to design projects that really matter to the students. Most often, projects are designed to answer some important questions and to affect people. The project is not merely an end in itself; rather, it is to mean something to someone, including people other than those involved in doing the project. Teachers have overall goals in mind, and they are able to help the students understand why the particular project is significant to them, but the students have much say in just how they will accomplish the goals and complete the task.

Students may work alone, but at times they must also cooperate with one another. They learn to work together, and they take time to deal with personal difficulties or conflicts. No one is allowed to dictate or produce all the work, and no one is allowed to be silent and contribute nothing.

When a product is the appropriate outcome of the project, students generally know how they will be evaluated before they begin. But the product is not the sole basis of the evaluation. Throughout the project, students and teachers consider what kind of evaluation will be appropriate, and teachers provide students with regular feedback. Students design the product to accomplish more than a display of knowledge they have gained. They may use it to stimulate further exploration, to communicate with others outside the class, or to include it in an even larger body of information for others to use in the future. The product is not necessarily an end in itself.

Cooperation. We can readily see what an important role cooperation plays in learning in a classroom where students are treated as image bearers. Students and teachers cooperate to plan and monitor the learning activities, to pursue the goals and accomplish the tasks, and to evaluate the learning throughout.

The work groups are designed to maximize the learning of all students. Sometimes that means students with varying abilities are in a group because the more able students benefit from helping the less able, and the less able ones benefit from that help. Learning is not just about mastering content. It involves loving and serving one another and learning how to let oneself be served.

Sometimes groups are formed around interest, motivation, and need. In these groups, students learn the value of pursuing a common goal and the difference it makes to be of one mind in their work. Sometimes groups are formed by combining students who have certain skills and gifts needed to accomplish the task.

While it is not the sole means of learning, cooperative learning plays a prominent role. Individual learning and cooperative learning are designed to complement each another. And while students are held personally accountable for what they have learned (just as we are personally accountable to God for our own behavior and choices), they are also accountable for one another's learning (just as members of Christ's body are responsible for one another and for carrying one another's burdens). This degree of cooperation may seem contrary to our common experience, but then the kingdom of God is often contrary to the way we experience life in a fallen world.

Competition plays a very small role in learning from this perspective. In competition, there are always losers as well as winners, and contrary to popular belief, the losers (the ones who often have the most to learn) are seldom motivated to learn through competition. They know the likelihood of winning is small, and being constantly on display before your peers as a loser is hardly motivational in a positive way. Competitive learning games are used very sparingly, as the detrimental effects accrue even to the winners. It is all too easy for them to become self-satisfied in their accomplishments rather than to be concerned about the learning and benefits of the whole group. A positive identity built on winning and a negative one built on losing are hardly consistent with a biblical basis for identity.

Service. Many learning activities include a service component. Perhaps service is indeed the desired goal. Even if it is not, learning is connected with service to others as pervasively as possible. When students are engaged in a project, they often design it so that it benefits others who need it. Sometimes the first-grade students can benefit from fifth-grade students who listen to them read or read to them. When learning to use certain mathematical skills, students may contribute to the construction of some part of the playground.

Older students are better able to discern needs of others outside the school through exposure to the news, volunteer organizations, or personal acquaintances. As they discern those needs, they bring their newfound awareness to class, and teachers work with them to find ways to use their knowledge in meeting those needs. Perhaps a class project will arise. Perhaps it will simply be an individual working with needs in the city or neighborhood. In either case, those involved will be fulfilling their academic requirements.

Life outside the school. Learning activities should not be confined to what happens within the walls of the classroom. School should not become a world of its own, unrelated to what goes on everywhere else. Rather, what goes on inside the classroom should reflect what is going on outside. It should help students deal with what is happening in the rest of life. Therefore, students are often out in the community investigating things, talking with people and asking lots of questions, working with and for people, helping the needy, and learning from experts.

Such activity is never just an "add-on." Students do not take field trips or engage in activity outside the school just to get a break, or to have another kind of experience. Community activity is directly related to classroom activity. At times, student involvement in the community directs the inquiry and the class discussion since it provides the impetus for the particulars of the study. At other times, classroom discussion and learning leads to involvement in the community. The academic disciplines generate involvement outside the school, causing students to dig deeper into the academic disciplines in order to respond better.

Hands-on experience. Textbooks are viewed as guides and resources, not as the dictators of moment-by-moment experience. "Covering the text" is not equated with learning the material. Because teachers believe that to learn something means to have accepted it at a heart level, and because they realize that getting to the heart usually involves more than just using the brain, they encourage students to get involved in what they are learning—physically, emotionally, intellectually, and spiritually. Students must be immersed in what they are doing, not just reading about things.

Consequently, when students are learning to write, they write things that are significant to them and to others. When they learn to compute area, they determine how much grass seed the ball field needs and then plant it. When they study justice, they do not just visit a court or have a mock courtroom. They get involved in issues and causes that exist to bring about justice. As they learn to cook, they cook for someone who needs to eat. As they write poetry, they publish it for others to enjoy.

One sees little in the way of worksheets and practice sheets in classrooms where these principles are accepted. These are used when they might be helpful, but they do not consume much of the students' learning energies. Rather, students spend their time working with ideas, things, and people.

Meaningful tasks. Because we all channel our energy into what is meaningful to us, teachers realize they must determine what already means something to their students and build learning activities on that. They ask the students lots of questions; they observe them on the playground, on the ball field, and in the lunchroom. They make it a point to know the youth culture and home backgrounds of their students. Then they can intelligently engage them in discussion of learning activities that will not only pursue the goals that the teacher knows are important but do so in a manner that utilizes the motivations the students already have.

The teachers also find ways to encourage the students to have a sense of "the need to know." Students are not always mature enough to be aware of what they need to know, and often the felt needs that motivate them may not be the most significant for them to address. Therefore, teachers must become good at raising consciousness and creating the tension necessary to provide their students with a sense of the need to know.

Practically speaking, learning involves much input from the students. Teachers pay close attention to how they begin a particular learning activity. Problem solving is happening all the time, and the problems are some that students have come to see as worthy and meaningful, even if it is the teachers who have brought them to see the problems in that light.

Tasks that affect someone. Meaningful tasks are not only those that raise interest in the students; they also include those things that will matter to someone else. Learning activities should always be discussed in light of who will be affected by them and why that is important. Answers to those questions affect the design of the experiences. Seldom should teachers choose activities that will affect only the learner. Rather, teachers should choose activities and design them in part for their impact on someone with a need—whether an invalid, a senator, or a parent.

Open interactions. It should be clear by now that learning is not characterized by the storing up of information, nor by the completely sequential covering of academic material, nor by the performing of intellectual gymnastics. Learning should be characterized by open discussion, bold questioning, fearless exploration, humility in arriving at conclusions, acceptance of failure in the process, and faithful attempts at loving others through what is learned. Students and teachers are together in the learning process, and therefore they have to be open with one another and trust one another. Expertise is not held over the heads of the nonexperts. Instead, it is given freely and received freely. Those whose minds are already made up and who simply want confirmation of what they already know will not be comfortable in such an environment.

The Bible. Biblical principles and themes are always brought to bear on the problems the students attempt to solve, the service they seek to provide, the solutions and conclusions they reach, and the effects they hope to have on others. Any teacher can do what we have described up to this point, but only a Christian teacher is concerned with the application of biblical truth to learning. The themes and norms revealed in the Bible are always the foundation for asking questions, pursuing learning, engaging in the task, and evaluating solutions and conclusions even if they are not openly identified as biblical principles.

Quiet reflections. Few schools provide much reflection time. We are seldom given the opportunity to actually think on the implications of what we have done. Students should be regularly given time to ponder, wonder, and reflect on what is going on around them, on who they are, and on what is happening in the world. Reflection time may occur before, during, or after a particular learning activity. Journaling is one means of promoting such reflection, but whatever means is used we see that learning is not just an activity; learning includes internal reflection on its meaning.

How Is This Grace at Work?

It treats the learner as an image bearer. When we consider what it means to be created in the image of God, the learning tasks described seem to do that. Solving problems and serving others require the students to think creatively. The types of projects described give students opportunities to exercise dominion. By dealing with real questions in the world around them, they confront moral decisions that they must make.

The kind of input that students have in determining the nature and course of the learning activities indicates that teachers acknowledge the freedom and responsibility of image bearers. When teachers ask students to act on what they believe as a part of the experience, the teachers recognize that the students are creatures of faith who are called on to exercise that faith. Cooperative efforts encourage students to fellowship with one another and to depend on one another while working together. Many of the projects and tasks give students the opportunity to be loving and merciful as they meet others' needs.

How do such learning activities recognize and deal with the fallen nature of the students? Have we ignored the effects of sin when we focus so much on the created attributes of God's image bearers? I do not think so. If we believe that the fall marred the image but did not destroy it, and that God's call for us to rule with Him and to reflect His character was not rescinded but misdirected, we must treat the students in ways that allow them to display that image and to pursue that calling. If we do otherwise, we fail them and God by giving sin too much power. Therefore, our attempt to live by the structure of God's creational norms is a recognition of the true nature of the fall rather than a misunderstood and exaggerated view of it.

Furthermore, an emphasis on encountering and serving others is a direct means of trying to deal with the estrangement and broken relationships caused by the fall. It also is a means of viewing and living life in a less self-centered way. As they work closely with the teacher, students deal with both their own insecurities and their self-centered orientation to life.

The framework reflects grace. If we extend grace while conducting learning activities, we demonstrate that we are willing to accept the mistakes and failures that result from our fallen use of our God-given creativity and rationality. Those failures and mistakes are part of what we can expect. If we allow students to fail and let them know that they are still loved, treasured, trusted, and allowed to try again, we demonstrate grace. Correcting them is not out of bounds, however. In fact, correcting students in a loving way is also an act of grace. But learning that occurs in an atmosphere of applause for success and punishment for failure breeds a performance identity.

Giving all students, not just the bright and successful ones, the right to explore and to be responsible for their actions is also an act of grace. It is not grace to provide able and dependable students with learning activities that allow them to be creative, caring, and responsible, while providing the less able and less dependable students with seat work that has no meaning or effect on other human beings. That is privilege based on performance. The students earn, or lose, their reward on the basis of how well they do.

Facing and accepting the limitations of students and ourselves as we pursue solutions to problems and prove them inadequate for the task is another demonstration of grace. When students do not succeed, they often feel shame and guilt. They sense that they have let themselves, or perhaps someone else, down. Indeed they have. But in an atmosphere where shortcomings of everyone (teachers included) are freely admitted, and where people are accepted anyway, students can find forgiveness and acceptance rather than shame and guilt.

Grace in learning activities also does not force students into one correct (or "pat") answer. It acknowledges the worthiness of an answer that does not seem to fit the norm, deals with different answers in humility, and attempts to take each answer as the stepping-stone to a new question and a new pursuit. Grace is not afraid to point out errors and show the dangers of following certain conclusions, but it does not simply judge responses as right or wrong and assign a grade. Learning activities should not be primarily merely to assign grades anyway. The teacher who uses assignments and tests and other learning activities only to have sufficient numbers of grades to report to parents fails to exhibit an acceptable purpose for learning, let alone learning in an atmosphere of grace.

Believing that children can indeed care for the creation, and giving them opportunities to do so, is an act of grace, for such a belief counters every sinful act we see children commit. We easily tend to think that they are not yet able—they are too selfish or foolish, or they cannot make a real difference. In other words, we sell them short. We do not give them what God gives them—the right and responsibility to rule over the creation with Him, even as children. A gracious God permits five-year-olds the rule that is appropriate, even when they do not always handle it correctly. Why should we do less? Do we do any better with what God gives us as adults?

Can we assume that children are able to love others when they are so obviously self-centered? Do we not have to restrain their sinful desire to please the self and to be lazy and uninterested in serving or loving others? Grace says, "I know all those tendencies, and I am going to give you the opportunity and challenge to love someone else anyway. Because the Spirit of God is at work here, I call on you to trust Him to be at work in the spirits of those selfish children and to use the experience to transform them into children who trust Christ."

Thus, children must be given the opportunity and challenge to love others even though their motives and actions will undoubtedly be inadequate in doing so. Jesus works with their efforts to love, even though those efforts are not perfect. We demonstrate that to them when we work with their efforts to love others also. If Jesus were to work with us only when our love was pure enough to warrant His presence, we would never see Him. Likewise, if we wait for students to have pure enough motives in serving others, we will never be able to let them serve. Instead, we are to demonstrate love for those who are still learning how to love others, knowing that our motives are no better than theirs.

Students who attempt to be reconciling agents are certain to have unwilling attitudes and to make mistakes. We are not very good at this endeavor ourselves. But God never takes away the calling to be reconcilers. In fact, He very clearly gives us that responsibility in spite of our bad attitudes and inept performance (2 Corinthians 5:18). We can keep on because He is with us, sanctifying our feeble attempts and overhauling our bad attitudes through His loving patience and the finished work of Jesus. He simply will not give up on us—that is clearly an act of grace. So should be our work with students.

According to grace-less thinking, this whole perspective is not very realistic in a fallen world. People are just not capable of achieving those purposes, and believing that they are capable would be folly, a failure to admit the depth and breadth of sin in human life. The best we can do is to control students and to restrain their sinful behavior, giving them learning tasks that will expose them to God's truth and trusting that He will someday change their hearts so that their lives might be more pleasing to Him.

Grace-full thinking is quite different. The purpose of education that would arise from biblical norms still stands. Because of sin we cannot please God solely with our efforts, but because of Christ, we are able to understand the biblical norms and pursue them, inept and self-centered as we may be. Through grace, Christ takes that pursuit and our fallen motives and weak performances and transforms them into something acceptable and pleasing to God. It is His righteousness that is acceptable, and that righteousness has been given to us.

God never stops dealing with us as He created us to be (indeed an act of grace), and He calls us to do the same with our students. As we do so, we reflect who He is. As we trust in Christ alone, not only for our salvation but also for making our educational efforts acceptable to the Father, we testify to His grace, for there is no other way we would dare attempt to educate according to His norms knowing how far short we fall in living up to them. Only one who is mad, or one who truly trusts Christ, would attempt to educate children God's way.

Now What?

What learning activities and assignments could you make that would reflect an effort to better treat your chosen students as image bearers and thus reveal a part of what grace is about?

13 Measurement, Evaluation, and Grading

The ways in which measurement, evaluation, and grading are handled are key to whether students will pursue the learning activities with integrity, purpose, and fearlessness or with little more than concern for a grade they will receive for their efforts. For very broken students, from very broken backgrounds, typical approaches to grading mean very little. Grades have long since been discarded as any means of identity, worth, or meaning. Hence, a very different approach is needed. Again, what would it look like in a classroom where the teacher believed and acted upon our convictions?

A Different Perspective

Grades downplayed. As difficult as it is to do in our modern culture, teachers must seriously attempt to downplay the perceived importance of grades. Because teachers must recognize the errors they can make in evaluating, they must place limits on just what grades are supposed to mean. And because they recognize the inevitable subjectivity of even the most conscientiously objective grading schemes, they do not delude themselves into thinking the grades they assign to student work are as valid and reliable as most would like to think.

One way in which this happens is that not all work has a grade placed on it. Work that is of a highly personal, controversial, open-ended, or ill-defined nature usually has only teacher comments, suggestions for further thought, and questions on it when it is returned to the students. Since the tasks the students engage in are seldom meaningless or just busywork, their motivation to do the work is not as tied to a grade they will receive. In fact, attaching a grade to meaningful work of the sort described above would likely hinder the honest, free pursuit of the task.

Failure accepted. The outlook on failure is quite different than at typical schools. Teachers operating from grace view failure (not ultimate failure but failure along the way) as an expected part of the learning process. Because the learning tasks are sizable, important, and difficult, students cannot expect to "get it right" at every point along the way. Failure is used in these instances as a step toward ultimate mastery and understanding. Thus, failure is a temporary, and admittedly often painful, part of the journey to success. It is significant that failures occurring as part of the learning process are not recorded and used later to penalize or punish students.

Multiple opportunities to achieve given. This attitude toward failure comes in part from the conviction that students should be given multiple opportunities and means to learn and to demonstrate that they have indeed learned. It is not a "one chance and too bad if you fail" environment. Sometimes teachers ask students to improve their work according to suggestions from the teacher or their peers. At other times, teachers allow students to pursue the task and produce evidence of learning in a manner that is different from the original design. In a classroom with an atmosphere of grace, students are safe to openly share their work with one another for critique, and they may turn in several drafts before they themselves, or the teachers, are satisfied.

Criteria for evaluation identified up front. So that students know what is expected of them in their often very flexible and fluid learning environment, teachers and students frequently (though not always) decide together what criteria should be used to evaluate the learning, and they publish those criteria for common understanding before the learning task even begins. The criteria should not be written in stone, for teacher and student alike may realize along the way that they made a bad choice for evaluating. In addition, not all evaluation must necessarily fit within the predetermined parameters.

Teachers and students determine the evaluation criteria at the outset of the learning activity, and they use those criteria for the process as well as the final product. They take accountability seriously, and everything does not hang on the quality of the product. This method makes it much harder for someone to float along until the very end since a student is not likely to produce a great result by paying little attention to it along the way. Those who work hard and do all they should, yet do not produce a superior product, will not be unduly penalized. Also, students who know how they are doing throughout the process will not be surprised or make excuses in the end. This type of evaluation will keep students on the path since it is fairly constant. We must be careful, however, that the evaluation design is not the ruling factor in determining the learning activities.

Self-evaluation and evaluation by peers implemented. Evaluation is not the exclusive domain of the teachers. While the teachers are ultimately responsible for assigning grades, they do not assign them without considerable input from the students.

Teachers encourage individual students to monitor their effort and achievement throughout the learning task. Since most tasks are of some duration, students can easily include details of their work. Sometimes they report on what they have done, how they have gone about it, and what they think they have learned from it. At other times, they may be asked to judge the quality of their own work according to the criteria determined at the outset. They often use journals to supplement the more objective process, since in the journals they write about learning and processes that may not seem so directly connected to the assigned task but that are nevertheless important to them. When it is appropriate, teachers consider what students have to say about their own learning by interacting with them orally or in writing before giving them a final evaluation and assigning a grade.

Students are expected to help one another through peer evaluation as well. If the learning takes place in a community in which people love and serve one another, the prospect of failure is not so embarrassing or shameful. Because all the students are pushed beyond their limits and fail somewhere, the stigma of failure is lessened. And because they often accomplish the learning only through cooperating with one another, students have no reason to belittle classmates and every reason to listen to them and help them. Again, by working together before the learning activity begins, teachers and students determine the process of peer evaluation and the criteria they will use. But either the teachers or students may modify the process and criteria as they see fit.

Observations conducted in various situations. Teachers observe students at work and in various situations to note evidence of their learning. They may have some formal checklists of the behaviors that demonstrate learning, but informal anecdotal-type records are just as important. As much as possible they conduct these observations in real-life or lifelike situations so that students do not merely attempt to give teachers what they want. Teachers sometimes discuss their observations with students since students can potentially learn from the experience. In this way, students are challenged to reflect on what they are learning, not just the final product and the grade they receive.

Portfolios used. Such an approach to evaluation lends itself to the use of portfolios to demonstrate student learning and achievement. While there are perhaps many ways to develop portfolios, the idea is to compile evidence of student work that can be used to demonstrate learning. Actual pieces of the students' work and samples of students' performance on various learning activities are included as evidence of learning—for instance, essays, drawings, solutions to various problems, and project abstracts.

Artists and photographers carry portfolios of work to show visible evidence of their abilities. Students may use their portfolios to show their parents what they have learned and to keep a personal record of their learning. Older students may use their portfolios when they apply for jobs.

The students usually select items for inclusion in the portfolio, but the teacher may at times have a specific reason to ask them to include a particular piece of work. The portfolios are not necessarily used to generate a final grade, though they sometimes play a part in determining it.

Assessment in real situations given. Since teachers ask the students to be involved in many real-life situations, they have opportunities to include the students' involvement and performance in these tasks as a part of their evaluation. Learning measured in true-to-life situations is normally much more valuable than that measured in ordinary school situations. In real-life situations, the criteria may not be easily defined and may be very subjective. Because teachers and students alike understand and accept this fact, it is a worthy means of evaluation rather than simply a reason to get upset because the criteria are not so clearly laid out.

This type of assessment rarely leads to a grade, as with some other types of assessment already mentioned. Oral and written feedback applied to the students' lives is much more important to students than a grade. In fact, attaching a grade to such an evaluation might ruin the learning experience because if the grade becomes the motivation for doing the task, students lose the experience of doing the task for its own sake.

Tests constructed and used carefully. If teachers construct and use tests as they should, students are not afraid of tests, nor do they let them rule their lives. Teachers carefully construct the tests so that they relate to the course content and the way it has been taught. Students do not study grand ideas and then have to deal with minute facts and events on the test. They do not deal with one set of ideas or skills in class and then find themselves tested on ideas and skills that come from some other mysterious place.

Teachers construct tests that enable them to measure what the students have already learned, but they also design them so that further learning occurs when the students are taking the test. The test itself is viewed as another learning experience. Questions are clear and fair, but often open-ended—especially when the learning activities themselves are open-ended. The questions deal with important topics and skills, and they do so in ways that cause the students to use their minds rationally and creatively according to their stages of development. Tests would often require students to go further than they have actually gone in class, but gently so. Learning requires students to stretch, and tests are acceptable places to do that stretching.

This practice is acceptable because of how teachers use the tests at the school. Tests are not the final, or sole, determiners of student evaluation. Students have opportunities, or sometimes they are required, to redo tests—better justifying what they said, doing alternative problems, fixing the things they did wrong the first time. With the aim of doing whatever will increase the students' learning the most, the teachers and students determine the particular means of dealing with failure or insufficient performance on the test. But they do not simply give the test, record the result, and move on regardless of the outcome.

It would not be considered unusual for students to design their own test questions. Teachers could trust students to do that, and students trust teachers to select carefully and to weed out or revise poor questions when necessary. Teachers do not always think of the most important things to ask on tests, and students do not always see what is most important either—another reason why, and another means through which, students and teachers work collaboratively in the classroom.

Teachers also place tests in an overall assessment and evaluation program to ensure that they are weighted appropriately in terms of the overall evaluation and report of the learning. There would never be a policy that says, "Three tests make up the final grade." There would be multiple opportunities to measure learning, and testing is only one of them. It is not judged to be more or less important than some of the other means such as observations, portfolios, and self-evaluation. The teacher values the contribution of well-designed tests to learning and the measure of learning, but the teacher does not elevate tests and their results to a status that they do not deserve.

Teachers should use standardized tests with restraint and common sense, and they should not use the results to compare their students to others or to place children in learning slots. Since locally developed tests (including classroom tests developed by the teacher) are carefully constructed to measure student learning against goals determined by the school, they are much more significant. Standardized tests may be used to give teachers, parents, and students some idea of where the students rate in performance with others who take the tests, but if teachers follow their own agenda as set by God, they recognize the inherent limitations of applying a standardized test result to judge any school or student.

Why This Perspective?

The learner as a fallen image bearer. The fallen nature of human beings and the way God deals with us give us considerably more reason to be tentative and formative in our approaches to evaluation. Limitations and sinfulness are ever before us. The key to life, however, is not to somehow through careful planning and pursuit of learning overcome the limitations and eliminate the sin. That is the approach of the law. The approach of grace in dealing with the learners insists that any performance is an offering of thanks to the God who saved us in spite of ourselves, and even that offering must be cleansed by the blood of Christ if it is to be acceptable to God.

This recognition of who we are demands that neither failure nor success be absolutized, the marks of our evaluation etched permanently in our being for all to see. For we are not judged, accepted, or used by God according to our failure or success. Rather, we are called to bear His image even though we, in our sin, will do it poorly and at times harmfully. In that process, He continually affirms us because of Christ. The evaluation and grading approach used by a Christian teacher is meant, however weakly and falteringly, to reflect that truth.

It is worth mentioning again that just as the purpose of education does not lend itself well to an objective, scientific measurement of achievement, neither does the human being. We are not defined by all that we can see and measure. There is more to us than science can deal with or understand. There are also things about us that only God and we ourselves can see. Thus, the matter of self-evaluation before God is significant. Because we are dependent beings created to love and support one another in the body, the evaluation and feedback of our peers and colleagues is valid and necessary. And because human beings were created to live in the world, it seems necessary to evaluate how we are doing in that very world, not in an unnatural environment. (And schools can sometimes be just about the most unnatural environment in which students will find themselves.)

The teacher as a fallen image bearer. The approach to evaluation and grading discussed also recognizes the frailty, limitations, and sinfulness of the teachers. Since they cannot be trusted to do it well enough, teachers cannot simply pronounce some absolute evaluation on their students. They must be tentative, flexible, willing to be corrected through input from others and to depend on that input as well. That is why the students participate in their own evaluation and the evaluation of others. It also is why they have multiple opportunities to demonstrate learning.

To help students and teachers evaluate the same concerns in the same way as much as possible, they discuss the evaluation criteria at the outset and make decisions about it before the learning begins. This preliminary discussion is another way of dealing with the frailty of both students and teachers.

This approach, however, does not exist simply to deal with the fallenness of the teachers. It also exists to let them live out the image of God—to be creative, rational, free, and responsible; to exercise proper dominion; and to recognize their limitations and dependence as creatures. This kind of participation truly allows them to be who God created them to be. It allows them to again fulfill the kingly role as a servant rather than as a tyrant, the priestly role in dealing with failure, the prophetic role in actually making judgments about learning the quality of student work, and the shepherd's role in leading the students to truth by evaluating where they are now and where they should go.

The nature of grace. Perhaps in no other dimension of school life is it more difficult to put grace into practice than evaluation. This is the place where students must in some fashion perform and be judged by their performance. School is also where others are likely to accept or reject one on the basis of performance, and thus it is also where students will form an opinion of their *self* that is based on something other than the righteousness of Christ.

Clearly, we may be tempted to suggest doing away with measurement, evaluation, and grading in order for grace to operate. Such a conclusion does not necessarily follow, however, when we look at some biblical teaching on the way God deals with our performance.

God has standards, and He demands that we live up to them. His laws are not merely suggestions. He causes us to evaluate ourselves as we examine our own lives against His laws. We know when we are doing better or worse through self-examination and interaction with others. Jesus Himself did not hesitate in evaluating the work and attitudes of both His disciples and His enemies. He gave them pretty clear feedback about how they were doing according to God's standards. So we need not avoid the evaluation of our students' outward work or of their inner attitudes. The question comes in trying to understand just how God's evaluation of us reflects the nature of grace.

First, while God evaluates (and helps us evaluate) the ways in which we do or do not live up to His law, He continually allows us new opportunities to try again. His mercies are "new every morning" (Lamentations 3:23), His patience is unending, and His desire that we keep on is eternal. Measurement and evaluation plans that allow students to try again, to get a new slant and make another attempt, to learn from their failure and make corrections reflect an attitude of grace. Systems that tend to treat performances as final products that mark a student once and for all do not reflect much grace. Approaches that are more formative, not just allowing but expecting revisions and renewed attempts, are much more grace-full.

Second, God's evaluation is meant to cause us to look at ourselves *and* at Him. Since we are fallen, our evaluations will always show us coming up short. Our shortcomings need not cause us to despair, though, for when we come to that realization in an atmosphere of grace, we are brought to look at the one who clearly loves and accepts us in our lack of performance. We see one who does not affirm or deny us on the basis of our performance but on the basis of His own love for us and of Christ, whose performance was flawless and credited to our account. That grace is demonstrated when teachers interact with students in ways that show they are loved and accepted, and when the teachers affirm their students' "being" apart from what they may do. The more students see teachers who love them whether they perform well or perform poorly, the more they will experience the reality that God loves them the same way. The less they see their standing in the eyes of the teacher as dependent on their grades, the more they will experience love from grace rather than performance (which is not really love at all).

When teachers take evaluations that show failure and mistakes and use them to produce eventual success, they demonstrate grace. God demonstrates His grace through the way in which He turns bad into good and mistakes into successes. That again is what redemption does. When teachers take poor student performance on one assignment and use it to help create success on the next (instead of merely punishing the failure with a bad grade), they reflect grace.

Teachers also show grace when they continually trust students to pursue new learning tasks that carry responsibility even after they may have failed at a previous task. For God does not remove us from the opportunity to live out His image even though we fail at it every day. On the contrary, He keeps thrusting us out into places where that image can be displayed again and again, sometimes *especially* in the places where we have failed. His desire is that we continue in His Spirit so that both the possible improvement and our continued effort testify to His grace. Thus, grace demands that students who fail at a task or responsibility be given that responsibility again and again, not have it taken away from them. And they will not be asked to take on the responsibility or perform the task alone without sufficient help from the teacher or others. Rather, as God sends His Spirit to us, He also sends His Spirit to them. And, as He calls for members of the body to go with one another into these responsibilities, so He calls for teachers and fellow students to help students who are having trouble accomplishing the learning task. Grace is thus demonstrated in a corporate sense, not just an individual one.

Finally, a reporting system that consists of evaluative comments rather than mere letter grades, and that reflects evaluation of the process as well as of the product, is justified by grace. In God's economy, the final evaluation has been placed on us. In Christ, we are given the eternal blessing before we even do anything. The evaluation that then helps us live in a fallen world as reflections of God is the one that takes place during the process. It does not consist of marks that show how we measure up against the standard. It consists of communication that reveals much about us and about the one who helps us pursue the standards. A reporting system that consists merely of grades communicates very little and reflects very little of how God evaluates and reports to us.

Now What?

What changes in your approach to measurement, evaluation, and grading could you make that would reflect an effort to better treat your chosen students as image bearers and thus reveal a part of what grace is about?

14 Classroom Behavior and Discipline

In a classroom where grace is in place, the behavior of students is ultimately determined by their own choices, and it is their personal responsibility. But classroom behavior is affected by a number of factors over which teachers have considerable influence—the way teachers view students, the way teachers view their own roles, the nature and meaningfulness of the learning tasks, the worthiness of the curriculum, even the purpose for which learning occurs. Classroom behavior is also influenced significantly by how committed the teachers and students are to one another, whether they have become a community, how failure is handled, and whether the atmosphere is one of grace and forgiveness or legalism and performance.

In this chapter, I have conspicuously omitted any reference to a classroom management system or highly defined approach to disciplining. Systems of rewards and punishments and means of controlling students so they behave appropriately reflect beliefs—about human nature, God's relationship with His people, and human relationships—that contradict the basic beliefs outlined in this book. Therefore, teachers are urged to consider a different perspective once again, so let's see what it looks like.

Interaction with Students

Realizing that rules are not the main thing. Classrooms that rely on imposing rules and regulations, coercing or enticing students into acceptable behavior through threat of punishment or promise of reward, and using carefully devised and executed "systems" of control are classrooms where the students are viewed primarily in terms of their fallen nature instead of as image bearers. Teachers in these classrooms think that the students will take a mile when given an inch and will abuse any freedom and responsibility the teacher gives them. Teachers assume that the students will be disruptive and perhaps destructive. The teacher's job is to control.

At the other extreme, when teachers focus positively and often exclusively on the created potential of students, they tend to ignore the fallen nature of those students. In this case, the teachers assume that when students are trusted, they will naturally be trustworthy. When given freedom, they will use it responsibly. When allowed to make choices, they will make the right ones. This positive (often referred to as "humanistic") view of students sees them as needing only freedom and nurturing to blossom into the good flowers that they naturally are.

As a better approach, teachers view the students as fallen, yet still as image bearers of the living God. Viewing them as image bearers forces teachers to remember that they must treat the students as the free, responsible, creative, rational, moral corulers of the creation that God made them to be. It also forces them to realize that apart from the intervention of God through His Word, His Spirit, and His representatives of Christ, those students will inevitably live out that image in ways that do not honor God and that often hurt others. Therefore, as teachers who represent Christ, they enter the students' lives as incarnations of the truth, not to control students but to nurture, love, and discipline students in their fallenness. There is freedom, but it is exercised within a proper structure.

Moving beyond compliance. Teachers do not use their God-given authority simply to force students to comply with their rules and expectations or the school's. Neither do they use their authority to entice good behavior by rewarding it with approval or higher status. The emphasis is on people rather than rules.

Rules do exist for the better functioning of a large group of people living in proximity to one another, but the rules are never applied apart from consideration of the students and their circumstances. Students don't follow the rules just because they are the rules. Students are not treated as mere objects of the rules. When the rules appear to be unhelpful or possibly even harmful, they are set aside. *People* determine what will happen to people. Rules do not.

Teachers grant students responsibility and accountability so they can learn from mistakes and so that true forgiveness can be granted. Teachers do not overlook bad behavior or ignore mistakes. Rather, since they view students as image bearers who make choices, students are responsible for their choices. When students choose not to live up to their responsibility, or hurt someone else, they are accountable and they will be confronted with the behavior and the choice. Only real crimes can be granted real forgiveness, and the students are treated with enough dignity to call a crime a crime. When they confess to the crime, they warrant forgiveness, not merely punishment. Such is the grace of God at work.

Students are affirmed regardless of their behavior. The teachers do not have a program that draws attention to good or bad behavior in ways that motivate students to desire the affirmation that comes from behaving well. Good and bad feelings are expressed openly, and thus the persons having those feelings are affirmed in their right to have them. That does not mean the feelings are justifiable or righteous. It merely acknowledges the truth that someone has them.

God handles such feelings from us, so we should handle them from one another. He allows us to come to Him with our corrupt attitudes, feelings, and behaviors—perhaps one of the major ways in which we understand and experience His grace, since His affirmation so clearly cannot depend on whether our behavior is good enough. It clearly is not, but He affirms and accepts us because of the righteousness of Christ.

As teachers do the same for students, they testify once again to the reality of the gospel and thus operate out of a framework of grace. No student's behavior is ever completely acceptable, as even the purest of human motives are tainted with sin. And the behavior of very broken students is rarely close to acceptable. Thus, affirmation of all students is to be given because of Christ's work and because of who God made them to be; it is not dependent on their ability (or lack thereof) to behave according to the standards.

Building true community. Community is built through relationships. Since God exists in relationship within the Trinity, He created us to be in relationships also. Work, worship, and play—all are to be experienced in fellowship with others. Thus, relationships are important in any classroom. How do we go about building and maintaining such relationships?

The ways in which teachers and students participate together in planning learning activities, evaluating learning, and confronting problems in and out of the classroom all suggest that there is a mutual respect among the various participants. Teachers respect the students by including them in the decision making, listening to them, and acting on their suggestions. Students respect one another by helping one another, depending on one another, and trusting one another to help solve real problems. Students respect the teachers by listening to them, trusting them to lead and care for them, and being committed to pursuing the learning goals and tasks even when they do not immediately see the relevance of them. (To do so suggests the students indeed have come to trust the teachers.)

Students and teachers are allowed and expected to connect with one another in regard not only to academic tasks but also to personal concerns. The classroom is not a place for group therapy, but it is a place for people who trust one another to make known their concerns and issues and to be supported in them. Whenever personal problems arise among students or between the teacher and students as a whole, the class takes time to talk about them and tries to resolve them. When a particular student is having a hard time, others are allowed and encouraged to support that student even when it may mean taking up some class time. Teachers are also open about their own struggles in life (as is appropriate) and are willing to lean on the students for support.

The classroom community also looks for ways to serve one another. Time is allowed for discussions of how this might be done, sometimes in conjunction with a unit of academic study, sometimes in light of issues or problems that arise simply through living with one another for seven hours a day. It may involve students helping one another academically, supporting those with physical limitations, or sharing the responsibility of keeping the room clean. Teachers also ask the students to help them evaluate, plan, and think through problems.

Class meetings involve not only discussing curricular matters but also dealing with behavior and classroom decorum. Such meetings are more common than specific systems of rules and regulations. Because students are recognized as God's image bearers, their behavior is not managed by a program or a system. Rather, individual and whole class behavior is dealt with personally—whether that means discussion or the application of consequences to the behavior or both.

The incarnate Jesus, though having all authority in heaven and earth, left His position to become one of us and one with us. He experienced what we experienced, lived with us, served us, suffered for us and with us, taught and corrected us, and led us into an encounter with God and His grace. He offered, led, and taught, but He did not coerce or entice. He never violated our created being by treating us as less than human. This too creates community.

Therefore, students are trusted and given freedom and responsibility. They are not simply controlled, but they make choices about both behavior and consequences, they have some say about policies that will make the class operate more smoothly, and they are expected to deal with one another as God's crown of creation. This approach also means that when the fallen nature produces unacceptable behavior and mistreatment of one another, correction according to God's standard and forgiveness is extended to a repentant offender. Teachers are not afraid to stand firm in facing students who want to challenge their authority and cross the boundaries. Corrective discipline is applied as necessary, but always as a part of the grace given to the one who misbehaves. Students and teachers alike are also involved in determining how justice and mercy kiss in dealing with an offense.

Finally, teachers and students who are aware of their fallen nature realize that good outward behavior is not a sufficient measure of true godliness. In fact, outward behavior may become an insidious source of pride, and therefore a sin. "Good" students are not held up before others as examples to be emulated, nor is good behavior always applauded and rewarded. It is appreciated, but it does not become the source of affirmation of any individual. Students who behave well are asked to examine their motives and perspectives just as readily as those who behave badly. Again, this self-examination may come through class discussion or personal interaction with the teachers.

Interaction Worthy of Image Bearers

The learner. A classroom that operates like ones described above certainly demonstrates an effort to treat the students as image bearers. They are called on to be responsible as they exercise their freedom and dominion. They must relate to one another socially and learn to deal justly and mercifully with one another. Students also have opportunities to use their creativity. In fact, I suspect that all the characteristics of image bearing are utilized in the process.

The fallen nature of the students is not ignored. They are not left on their own to manage the classroom. A godly teacher is involved as their guide and authority. Neither teachers nor students are allowed to simply operate according to whim and feeling. Biblical teaching guides all attempts to set policies, to enforce them, to change them when necessary, and to set them aside when appropriate. Boundaries exist because students need them for security. Teachers deal with misconduct because students need to be loved.

Perhaps the most important fact about the whole process is that it seems to be designed to ask everyone—teacher and students alike—to act redemptively. The goal is always reconciliation, not mere compliance. The process is designed to affect the heart, to bring better commitments, to recognize and confess sin, and to experience forgiveness. The students do not just behave outwardly the way the teacher or the school wants.

The teacher. Teachers are to treat students as God treats them, as fallen sinners who are hopeless apart from His grace, but who are to be dealt with according to what He made them to be. Teachers are personal, not mechanical. They rely on the Spirit of God moving in the students and themselves rather than on management systems. They do not need to control as much as they need to shepherd.

The teacher's role as shepherd dramatically affects the approach to classroom behavior and discipline. The tools of the shepherd are his voice, his rod, and his staff. Also, many shepherds have a sheep dog. They do not have elaborate systems for managing their sheep, for sheep are not to be "managed." Rather, they are to be nourished, protected from harm, and brought to places where they can flourish— even though they are "dumb" creatures whose propensity is to go astray and get themselves into trouble.

The teacher's voice is familiar because it is used often in open, meaningful conversation, not simply at times when the student is about to wander off and go astray. Nor is it used simply to applaud good behavior. The teacher's voice also speaks comfort and assurance to the students. Comfort and assurance come in many ways, but one of the most important is through words of affirmation and encouragement— what we might call "pleasant" words. These words suggest that the sheep (students) are the shepherd's beloved no matter how they behave. They also call students back into the fold when they are wandering off.

The shepherd uses his rod to correct the sheep when they are creating trouble for others or themselves. When the sheep know the shepherd well enough, and they have learned that he is concerned only for them, the mere tap of his rod is enough to turn them away from folly. A word of warning may often be sufficient because of what has developed between the teachers and students. But the rod of discipline is used when necessary (whatever form that rod may take) to make known in no uncertain terms that students must not go further down the path to harm. To ignore this use of the rod is to carelessly allow the students to bring harm to themselves and perhaps the whole flock as they lead others astray with them.

The shepherd also uses his staff to comfort the sheep. With it, he draws the sheep together into an intimate relationship. He uses it to bring a newborn lamb to its mother should they become separated. Also, he uses it to draw the individual sheep to the shepherd for careful examination. And finally, he uses his staff to guide the sheep, laying it gently against the animal's side to direct it in the proper path (Keller 1970). The teachers' staff may again be words of encouragement, an arm around the shoulder, a touch on the head, an involvement in the life of the students outside the school, or whatever other means may be appropriate to create an intimate relationship with the teacher and the other students and to guide them in the paths they should follow.

The sheep dog assists the shepherd in moving the sheep to better pasture and keeping them there, in fending off harmful intruders, and in giving them a sense of peace. The sheep dog is totally loyal to the shepherd and the sheep, constantly at watch to ensure that the sheep are not harmed, and committed completely to the shepherd and the sheep (Keller 1983).

In some ways, maybe teachers are more like the sheep dog than the shepherd. Jesus is indeed the good shepherd of all the children who come into our classrooms, and perhaps we should see ourselves as simply His assistants. And though the metaphor may be stretched a bit far, perhaps the teacher's ability to structure meaningful learning tasks contributes to the peace of a classroom, so that the teacher can help to prevent the students from wandering astray in the first place.

Students involved in worthwhile activities are doing what they were created to do, and they therefore experience a sense of shalom. Good tasks are like good pasture, and involvement in meaningful service tends to fend off trouble as energies are exerted in positive ways. Whether or not the metaphor may be stretched too far, structuring the learning experiences through the use of meaningful tasks in a safe environment has a significant effect on classroom behavior. Teachers know that involvement in worthwhile things contributes significantly to the classroom decorum, and therefore they see to it that students engage in worthwhile experiences.

Grace, Not Law

The normal expectation for classroom behavior and discipline is to operate according to the law. Compliance with the law is good, and it is often even judged to be good enough. Following the law produces order, and order is good. Therefore, when our students follow the law, they are being good and things are good. How simple and "effective" would it be to adopt this approach were it not for the fact that it surreptitiously undermines the gospel.

As prescribed here, teachers are not fooled into thinking that compliance with the rules is good enough. They are not satisfied with mere compliance. They wish to teach their students that they can never find acceptance, assurance, or identity by simply keeping the rules, for in God's economy they can never keep the rules well enough to gain any of those things.

A final, and perhaps the most outrageous, thought on the subject of dealing with unacceptable behavior—inspired again by the reality of God's grace—is that because God loved His people and knew they could not turn from their sin on their own (dead persons cannot make choices for life), He chose to pay the price for their sin in order to make them whole again. He gave His own Son to satisfy the demands of His justice and sent His Spirit to empower and guide His children in righteousness. How do teachers emulate Him? Does teaching redemptively mean that teachers are somehow expected to "pay the price" for their students? What "spirit" do they have to give in order to inspire students to walk in righteousness?

Ultimately, of course, nothing a fallen teacher could give for a fallen student would satisfy God's justice; only Jesus can do that. But if we are to be living pictures of God, then perhaps we are challenged to think about the sacrifices we may need to make in order to show students what the sacrifice of Christ means to them. We may need to sacrifice efficiency, control, and comfort for ourselves (all of which most discipline and behavioral control systems provide) so that we can walk into the personal agonies of misbehaving children. If we are to understand and share in the pain of a child who is creating trouble for the teacher and everyone else, we must act like Christ, sacrificing our comfort to feel the child's pain.

Entering into the lives of troublesome children also causes us to sacrifice our sense of position and well-being. At times, correcting them may cause us to sacrifice our sense of being loved by them. Any effort to deal with problem children as true human beings instead of as objects to be controlled will cost us time and energy and will likely put us into a situation where we cannot be sure of the outcome (loss of human control of the situation). It may even cost us our reputations (or our jobs) if dealing with the children in these ways does not reap the results others demand.

And as for the "spirit" that might inspire and empower more acceptable behavior, again we cannot give that to our students in any ultimate sense. The Holy Spirit alone can give that, and He moves in a person's life as He will. But we can, and must, offer ourselves as living examples. We can explain why students must be expected to act in certain ways. And we can demonstrate what it means to pursue righteousness and fall short, as we do constantly.

A living example is perhaps not so much a person who does everything the way it is supposed to be done as a person who, out of gratitude to God, wants to do what is right but falls short and rests in the righteousness of Christ. That is grace. That is the gospel. That is redemption. Where do we find it demonstrated in approaches to discipline that are designed to control students and to force their compliance with righteous expectations? We do not find it because we cannot.

When we expect students to pursue the good, we invite them to pursue righteousness instead of the sinful urges that still plague them. The spirit to empower comes through the way in which we grant that power to students, by not focusing on what is wrong with them but instead attempting to tap into what is good in them—the image of God and, for the believers among them, the person of Christ who now lives in them. If we treat them as image bearers, we invite them, and expect them, to live as such—just as God does.

A student's spirit to pursue righteousness also comes through the teacher's acting as a shepherd to help the "cast" sheep to its feet, allowing it to live and flourish as God intended. A cast sheep is one that has rolled over onto its back and is unable to right itself. More than likely, the sheep has chosen a comfortable spot to lie down (as on soft grass in a hollow) and has unsuspectingly rolled a bit too far over. The more it flails and attempts to get up, the worse things get. If left for long, it will die as gases begin to build up in the rumen and circulation is shut off in the limbs. To right the cast sheep, the shepherd does not merely pick it up and set it upright. Rather, he must first roll it over on its side, talking gently to it, and then lift it up slowly, rubbing its legs to regain the circulation. When it is upright, the sheep may still lack sufficient equilibrium so that when it attempts to walk, it falls in a heap and needs to be picked up again. With sufficient time, encouragement, and patience, the sheep is up and happy, able to go on feeding and flourishing (Keller 1970).

Students who cause trouble in the classroom are often "cast" students whose souls need to be restored. Their fallen nature ensures that they will be downcast, in the pit, unable to right themselves and get going—sometimes because of poor choices but often just because they rolled over a bit too far when they were comfortable, or because some circumstances over which they had little control dumped them over. Teachers do not shout at such students to get up, stand up, and do right, for such action does nothing to "restore the soul" of a student. Rather, they do as a shepherd does. They always keep an eye out for such students so they can find them before it is too late, "rubbing" their sore limbs, speaking in encouraging tones even when rebuking, and picking the student up—not once but as often as necessary.

Now What?

What changes in your approach to classroom behavior and discipline could you make that would reflect an effort to better treat your chosen students as image bearers and thus reveal a part of what grace is about?

Part 5

Dealing with the Cost: How Do I Keep Going?

15 Intimacy with God

Being a Friend of God

Let me take the liberty to relate to you a very personal story of becoming a friend of God—my own story. While in some sense it may be unique to me, in another sense there may be some universal truth in it.

I became a true follower of Jesus when I was in graduate school in 1968. Since then I have been privileged to know and to work with a very large number of friends and colleagues who are great teachers and followers of Jesus as well. My knowledge of the Christian faith and life has been immensely enriched and shaped by my interactions with those folks. I have read countless books, had much exposure to the Bible, and listened to many good messages in the past forty-three years as well. I have developed a Christian worldview that I believe truly does at least influence (if not always penetrate!) the way I live.

But it has only been in the past several years that I have come to know something of what it means to be a *friend of God*. Somehow, in all my readings and listenings and working relationships, that dimension of the Christian life was either overlooked or underplayed, or I just plain missed it. I knew God as mighty, holy, full of mercy and grace, deeply concerned about justice, willing to give His Son for me, and all kinds of important things that I learned from my life in the Christian community. But friendship with God was just not part of it.

So, I have mused a good bit about the nature of this newfound friendship with God, how it came to be, and how it might be sustained. Not surprisingly, it all seems to be the divine reality behind what we know and experience in temporal, earthly, human friendships. Here are some of the results of that musing, beginning with some scriptural underpinnings that helped me understand my own experience.

Mention of God's "Friends" in Scripture

Abraham. "O our God, did you not drive out the inhabitants of this land before your people Israel and give it forever to the descendants of *Abraham your friend*?" (2 Chronicles 20:7; emphasis mine).

"But you, O Israel, my servant, Jacob, whom I have chosen, you descendants of *Abraham my friend*" (Isaiah 41:8; emphasis mine).

"You see that his faith and his actions were working together, and his faith was made complete by what he did. And the scripture was fulfilled that says, 'Abraham believed God, and it was credited to him as righteousness,' and *he was called God's friend*. You see that a person is justified by what he does and not by faith alone" (James 2:22–24; emphasis mine).

Moses. "The Lord would speak to Moses face to face, as a man speaks with *his friend*" (Exodus 33:11; emphasis mine).

"Since then, no prophet has risen in Israel like Moses, whom the Lord knew face to face" (Deuteronomy 34:10).

Jesus' disciples. "I no longer call you slaves, because a master doesn't confide in his slaves. Now *you are my friends*, since I have told you everything the Father told me" (John 15:15, NLT; emphasis mine).

What Are the Themes of Friendship Revealed Here?

There is open, honest, sometimes bold *conversation* going on between the Father and Abraham, the Father and Moses, the Father and Jesus, and Jesus and His disciples. If you look at the various conversations recorded in the cases of Abraham and Moses, you see them conversing back and forth, just like two people do. They always said what was on their minds, without fear, with the humans obviously trusting God with all their thoughts, emotions, and even actions (all the humans managed to mess up in some way at various times). In fact, we read of Abraham that he believed God and trusted Him enough to do what God told him to do even though it was going to mean, in earthly terms, the loss of everything he had longed for—for nearly a hundred years! That, James said, made him God's friend.

There are many conversations recorded between the Father and Moses. Here we really see boldness coming out in Moses. He was bold enough to object and tell God he was too scared to do what He asked. He was also bold enough to ask God to change His mind at times. Moses must have trusted God a great deal to speak to Him like he did, and in the end, when the conversation was over, Moses again trusted God enough to do what He asked, even when it seemed hopeless, and dangerous, to him.

So it appears that *trust* is a big part of this as well. God, even though knowing the limitations of the earthly creatures He had made in His image, trusted them enough to reveal to them important things. Jesus said to His disciples that He had told them all that the Father had told Him. He was trusting them with what His Father had trusted Him with, and that, even though they did not yet seem very trustworthy, was His basis for calling them His friends and no longer His slaves, or servants. And eventually, when the Holy Spirit was in them, they too trusted Him enough to do what He asked.

It also appears to me that in all these situations what is being conversed about, what is being trusted to each other, is what is *in the hearts* of the friends who are having the conversations. Sometimes what is being discussed is *what deeply matters* to the people involved. Other times it may be very ordinary and "earthy"—just regular stuff. But there is never any pretense of trying to present oneself in the best light. It is the people and what is genuinely going on inside them that is entrusted to the other person.

In any case, these conversations that lead to friendship are completely honest, they reveal what is in the hearts of the participants, and they are offered in the context of great trust. It seems to me this is what builds, and maintains, friendship between human beings and that those friendships, valuable as they are in their own right, are meant to be pictures of, and invitations to, a divine friendship with God.

Then the two conversing are clearly *unreservedly ready to receive and welcome each other* where they are and with what they have to say. There is no fear in either saying or hearing. And though we will not go into it here, they also are willing to respond to each other with action as well as words.

What Did This Mean to Me?

So, a few years ago I simply began to try being friends with God. I found places where I could be alone with Him and talk out loud to Him. They were also places where I could be quiet and undistracted enough to listen to Him. I found that He speaks through the Scriptures, through impressing things on my mind by His Spirit, and through His creation, which exists because of His spoken word. (I love the outdoors, and I have many times been instructed concerning truths about God, me, and the world that He has revealed to me through observing what is around me in creation.) Most importantly, I experienced *the joy of just being with Him*. Sitting under a tree with God is a very good thing, even when neither has much to say!

I became very bold and honest, telling Him whatever was on my mind—knowing that much of it was hardly righteous, but it was what was going on inside me and I decided I would trust it to Him. He responded—often with surprises, sometimes with silence, always with acceptance and welcome. There were some very unusual and interesting interactions and some very ordinary interactions—just like there are with my close earthly friends.

One day as I was walking in the mountains of Ireland at Glendalough and talking out loud to God, I was simply stopped in my tracks and I exclaimed, "You know, God, I am not afraid of You anymore! The evidence of that is the way that I can talk to You about anything and everything and know that I am fully and eagerly received, and that You trust me enough to respond with what is on Your heart for me. You have really become my friend." I have not been the same since.

Saying Yes to God's Invitation

God has offered us an incredible invitation to enter into intimate relationship with him. Relationship. Loving connection with the One who sketched out the first atom, hung the stars without string, and crafted your soul with greater love than your mom felt as she knitted your first booties. Connection with the One who loves you with the romantic love of a groom for his bride.

Romantic? Yes. God's desire for love is stronger than your own, and his use of loving imagery in describing it is enough to make a bartender blush. The foreshadowing backdrop to Jesus' first miracle is a week-long wedding celebration in Cana. He leaves his apprentices with the charge to become one with the Father, and he calls the church his bride and himself the Groom. A bride invited to be at the greatest wedding celebration in the history of the universe, the Marriage Supper of the Lamb.

It boggles the mind. Why would God want to develop a loving relationship with me? What do I have that he doesn't already have at 10^{40}? What's in it for him? This can't be right! Even my spouse and kids need a break from being with me. Could the Creator of heaven and earth really desire to be my friend? my lover? closer than newlyweds on their honeymoon night? And forever and ever? Wow!

It's difficult for me to wrap my brain around the fact that I am not just saved *from* but *to*, that I'm saved to restored intimacy with God. With salvation comes an invitation to join in with the Trinity as part of their eternal community of love. And with it the offer to enjoy intimate fellowship that surpasses what is possible in the best of marriages....

With this staggering possibility, however, comes a sobering observation. Most marriages to Christ never get consummated. Most never experience the joy of union. Why? I believe it's because we fail to pursue him with the same reckless abandon with which we chased (or will chase) our spouse. We settle for brief encounters instead of intimate dialogue and become content with the contract instead of enjoying communion. Or perhaps the notion of viewing God in a romantic way frightens us, as does the possibility of losing the boundary of our self in the ocean of his love. (Moon 2004, 3–4)

This invitation is for all those who have said yes to Jesus' saving grace. It is not just for the super-spiritual, or the mystics. As Gary Moon suggests in *Falling for God: Saying Yes to His Extravagant Proposal* (2004), to accept this invitation is to embark on a relationship of honest *conversation, communion* coming from total commitment, and *consummation* that unites us with Christ so completely that we become living evidence of the incarnation. To say yes to this invitation is to begin to live fully in the love of the one who issues the invitation.

Maintaining That Relationship

Maintaining such an intimate relationship requires *togetherness*. When we seldom find ourselves together, the connection begins to fade, we begin to drift, the conversations become less open and honest, and intimacy begins to grow cold just as it does in human relationships. There is no real substitute for being together.

Prayer. Just as in human relationships, together does not necessarily mean physically together; it means hearts that are knit together. And how does my heart stay knit together with God's? First it would be through *prayer*—that special time when God and I get to share with each other what is on our hearts. Prayer cannot simply become a matter of my asking God for things and thanking Him for them when He "comes through" (what we call *answering our prayers*). Prayer is my opportunity to have special fellowship with Him. And I need more than a quick stop to acknowledge Him on my way out the door to do His work.

Most of us who have courted spouses and eventually wed them managed to create special, extended times together, when no one or no thing could distract or interrupt us. We often found special places to go that were just "ours." We did not go there with anyone else, because this was our very own place, where we had the opportunity and freedom to know each other as we had in no other place.

And, we kept going there. One visit, or very infrequent visits, was not enough. We returned again and again; and each time, though the surroundings were familiar, there was some new dimension to the experience that so fully satisfied us—even if that meant a time when neither of us had much of anything to say. We were just together, and that was enough.

So it needs to be with prayer. Yes, daily conversation with God is imperative, but it is not enough. He desires that we come home to Him to be alone with Him. He longs for us, as Richard Foster says in *Prayer: Finding the Heart's True Home* (1992, 1), and He wants all of us—not only the superficial parts. One of the keys to intimacy with God then is prayer, prayer that allows us extended time with Him, in a special place with Him, and that occurs with regularity and rhythm. Interestingly, I find that when I revel in these special times I find it much easier to see and experience His presence, involvement, and love for me in daily, earthy tasks. Awareness of Him all the time is enhanced by the special times of attention I give Him.

What does this prayer look like? In the previous excerpt from Richard Foster's book (in chapter 5), Foster tells us what this prayer looks like. It is far more than our placing our petitions and intercessions before God. Prayer is the language of intimacy between the two lovers—God and His people. This kind of prayer consists of *conversation*. It is just like returning to our earthly homes when we have been away for a time. When we first arrive, we are greeted with a warm welcome, likely a big bear hug. We are invited to the living room to sit for a while and make ourselves comfortable, have something to drink, and catch up on the family and what has been going on since we saw each other last. This, believe it or not, is a first step toward intimacy with the Father—sharing with Him what has been happening to us, what we have been thinking, what we are happy about, what we are sad about, what life has been like for us since we talked last. Then, the conversation in our earthly homes usually turns to asking the host in the home, "And what has been happening in your life? What has been on your heart lately?" If we have never conceived of talking to our Father this way, we should start now.

Next, the conversation may well move to the kitchen as the evening feast is being prepared. We eagerly ask about what is cooking and begin to anticipate with great delight what may be in store for us. The smell is enticing, and as Foster says, the "chatter and batter mix in good fun" (1992, 1). In an earthly kitchen, we usually ask whether there is anything we can do to help, and in many earthly kitchens the answer is usually, "No, I have it all under control." In our Father's kitchen, however, He is very likely going to invite us to take the "salad fixin's" and create a salad out of them. Or He may say, "If you have a favorite dessert recipe, help yourself to whatever I have and go for it. I would love to eat whatever you wish to create for us." When in His kitchen, we are quite welcome to participate in preparation of the feast we will soon enjoy together.

Dinner conversation always includes some praise and thanksgiving for how delicious the meal is. It is a proper and enjoyable time to compliment the host. Such praise and thanksgiving are quite appropriate when our Father is the host too. And the food, of course, is delicious. We thoroughly enjoy the meal together. Conversations usually begin to touch on topics of more serious concern, and eventually we decide to move to another room to continue.

We may take our coffee or tea to the sitting room again, or perhaps the study, as the topics of conversation usually gravitate toward something deeper. When guests come to my home, they usually have questions on their minds and they desire to know what I may think about them. Sometimes there are troubling things; sometimes there are things that have just captured their thoughts or dreams or visions. Input from me, the host, is always sought. So it is when we go into the study of our Father's house after the satisfying enjoyment of the feast. We can ask important questions and interact over weighty things that occupy our minds and hearts.

Sometimes creative thoughts and plans and ways to go forth in new adventures and challenges arise from these conversations. We are in a place where we can creatively partner with our Father in pursuing our calling to live out His character that has been placed within us. We may be apprentices for a while, or we may even take the lead in these endeavors. In either case, time with the Father to think, plan, evaluate, and create are important parts of our being in the "workshop" that Foster refers to.

Eventually, when the evening has worn on, we find ourselves tired and in need of rest. In our Father's house, He does not show us to just any bedroom; He takes us to *His own*! In a bedroom, there are two main things that happen—sleep and intimacy expressed between lovers. This is where we can let all the guards down and rest totally in peace, and this is also where we will know and be known in the most complete and mysterious way. Nothing is held back on either part. We can be, as Foster says, "naked and vulnerable and free" (1992, 2).

I suggest that if we want to know the *intimate* love of the Father, this will be a common approach to prayer for us. And if we want to *live* in that intimate love, we will often return home to Him this way in prayer.

Work. Intimacy is also maintained with someone when we work together. Prayer gives us the context for working with God. Entering into His work also keeps us intimately involved with Him.

We are partners in God's workshop. The work He has given us to do is something we do together just as we do in talking with Him in prayer. There is a "senior" partner (the Holy Spirit) who knows the job, what must be done, and how to do it most effectively. The "junior" partner is one who has been given the same job but who has much to learn about doing it and, in fact, cannot do it alone (that would be us). The motivation, the power, and the courage to do it all come through the union with the senior partner. The freedom to fail and try again comes because the senior partner always has things under control and He will not let us quit nor will He fire us. He is eternally linked to us, so we always get to try again.

He has a great mind, and He loves to engage ours. Every act of the creative use of our minds receives His affirmation because He knows that creativity reflects the character of the Father. And that is one of the things He exists to help us do. When we do not use that creative mind well, He will instruct and even correct us. But He never tries to squelch the use of it just because we used it badly. His attitude is that if we are indeed partners, He wants our involvement, cooperation, engagement, and surrender to His lead in order to get the work done.

The things that we create in the classroom are never perfect, and He is quite aware of that. But, because of the union the Spirit has with the Father and the Son, He knows that what we produce will be sent to the Father through the Son and thus be purified and perfected. That is why He can tell us we do not need to be afraid to pursue the work. When offered to the Father through Jesus, it is spotless!

Rest. Finally, the Holy Spirit leads us in the *fellowship of rest*. He knows well our frailty and our weakness and knows that the Father intends for us to rest. Rest is not merely what we do when we are too tired to go on. Rest is meant to be a part of the rhythm of life as God created it, and it too keeps us intimately connected with God.

Rest for most of us, however, seems hard to come by. There is too much to do to rest. We live in a culture (even our Christian culture) that values productivity over nearly everything else, and rest does not feel very productive—there is little to show for it. It is also scary, for if we rest we may begin to examine what is going on inside us, and we may have to face our demons and empty souls—souls that are empty in part because we never take time to rest.

Jesus says, "Come to me, all you who are weary and burdened, and I will give you rest" (Matthew 11:28). He goes on to describe it as "rest for your souls." He must have something in mind besides vacation, though that is a very legitimate part of rest. God says through Isaiah, "In repentance [returning to me] and rest is your salvation" (30:15). "Come to me" and "in returning to me" are movements toward God Himself. Being in His mere presence appears to lead to rest. And that is precisely what He wants for us.

As the Spirit leads us into the presence of God, He leads us to rest. When we go only to *ask* God for things (which is certainly a good thing to do), or even when we go just to *thank* Him for things (also a very good thing to do), we will not necessarily find rest. Such prayer is perhaps more like labor (though a fulfilling and joyful kind) than rest.

Rest of the sort Jesus and Isaiah mention has to do with abiding in God, delighting in His presence, *trusting* Him with the time, and believing that He delights in our presence as well. The Holy Spirit is the one who helps us accept this as good, right, and pleasing to God. Without the Spirit's fellowship (partnering) in this, we will all too likely fall prey to the "productivity" and "performance" problems. In the Spirit, it is desirable and delightful to sit under a tree for an hour with God, without either of us having to say a thing. Being together is the blessing, and it is refreshing and restful. This is the "rest for the soul" and the "salvation" that Jesus and Isaiah talk about. Without the Spirit, we will be busy on the inside, regardless if we are sitting still on the outside.

Now What?

Describe your level of intimacy with God and also where and how you desire for it to deepen. What ideas in this chapter could perhaps help you?

16 Living in a Rhythm

The Overwhelming Task

No one needs to be reminded of how hectic and pressured life is. Teachers have their own variety of that malady. The workload alone is enough to consume all our time, and if we add family, friends, church, and community involvement, we have the recipe for becoming overwhelmed. Add particularly broken kids from very dysfunctional backgrounds, and we have a steep slide to burnout.

As I was preparing to graduate from the teacher education program at my university, one of my professors told us that if we did not spend seventy-five hours per week on our teaching work during our first year we were not doing our job. I received that with incredulity, and then I got my first job and found he was right!

I happened to be blessed to have a school situation in which I loved what I was doing. The students were great, my colleagues were great, the facilities were great, and the opportunities were great. And being young, zealous, and eager to succeed, I did not mind pouring myself into the job for seventy-five hours per week. I did not particularly enjoy grading papers, but the other components of the job gave me great joy. I particularly liked the opportunity to be creative in the way I approached my teaching and the freedom to pursue and experiment with what I had planned.

As positive as it was, after a while it began to take a toll on me. And as I looked around at my more experienced colleagues, I realized that many of them had learned to cope with the overwhelming nature of the task by teaching the same things the same way over again year after year, by maintaining a greater distance from their students than I thought helpful, and by developing a level of cynicism that made me grimace. (Eating in the teachers' lunch room became quite unpleasant, since the main topic of conversation was always complaints about students.) And this situation occurred well before so many state and national expectations of "standards" put such an increasing burden on teachers!

In short, if teachers are to "have a life," we need help in learning to deal with plates that are too full and that sometimes contain too many toxic ingredients in the food on the plate.

The Beauty of Rhythm

The practice of intentional "rhythm" in life was something that was not introduced to me until way too late in life. There were rhythms that I lived by but never thought about—the rhythm of night and day, three meals a day, school bells telling me when to change classes, nine-week grading periods, semesters, summer breaks, seasons in the year, and so on. Also, my own young children always functioned better when they were on a schedule. All these things occurred fairly naturally, but I did not understand their value nor did I apply the principle of rhythm to life as it grew more complex. Then, when life was beginning to feel completely out of control, I was given the opportunity to spend a few weeks in a monastic guest program at a Benedictine monastery.

My intent was to see what God would do with me if He had my undivided attention for an extended period of time. I had no idea what He was going to do with it. I am not a Catholic by theology or practice, so a great deal was new and somewhat confusing to me. What was *not* confusing, however, was the schedule of the day and the week. Each hour of the day was scheduled—beginning at 3:00 AM for a worship service at 3:20. By 8:30 AM, I had been to three thirty-minute worship services, had two ninety-minute times of individual meditation and prayer, and had a silent breakfast. Then we went to work. Before silent lunch we had another worship service. In the early afternoon there was an hour for siesta. Then more work. Then more meditation time. Then more worship, silent dinner, more meditation, and a final worship service and time to end the day at 8:00 PM with complines.

When the schedule of the day was first explained to me, I thought would suffocate. I like to be the master of my own schedule and to determine what I will do and when. I could not imagine living by such a regimented schedule. But since I was there, I entered in as best I could. Within a matter of days, I found myself thoroughly enjoying every piece of the day. At some point I figured out why. I was not changing any of my beliefs, and I was still getting used to the worship liturgies. What I was experiencing was the incredible freedom of being able to enter *fully* into whatever was before me at the moment. I was not worrying about what had happened in the past, nor was I fretting over what might be coming in the future. The certainty of the structure allowed me to be *freely present and fully engaged* with every task, be it worship, work, prayer, food, or rest.

In ordinary circumstances I would find my mind flitting from here to there, thinking about this when I was in the middle of that. There was always the question of whether I would finish, and when I could not I would usually cheat the next person or event of some time to finish what had been currently going on. I spent much of my life being behind, yet thinking about what was coming ahead, and both guilty and angry about either. I could go through the day and wonder what had happened because I was so out of touch with most of it even while it was occurring. I did not really know what had happened, and then I felt frustrated because I had not accomplished anything that I could see. Only when a task was obviously completed, or a person was obviously helped, could I experience any satisfaction.

Even the lack of having to make a decision about every moment or every event is a benefit from rhythm. Those decisions add a burden to our day, they take energy, and they are not always easily resolved. A notable event at the monastery impressed that upon me.

Two of us were assigned to clean the guesthouse and screened-in porch for some important guests who were coming to visit. The monastery was going to approach them about funding a much-needed new library. We had about a two-hour block of time to work on this each afternoon of the week before an expected arrival of the guests on Saturday. As we attempted to clean the porch, we were given a pressure sprayer for the job. The pressure was great enough that it blasted the paint right off the cement porch, but of course not all of it, only pieces of it here and there. So blast, scrape, scrub—we tried it all and only succeeded in making it look worse. The afternoons rolled on, and each day the brother in charge came by to make sure we quit when the two hours was up so we could have the scheduled meditation time. There was no decision to be made.

The two of us who were working began to panic, but the monastery brothers showed no concern and they were not about to let us use some meditation time to work. The orders of the day were the orders of the day. By Friday we still had a mess, and the brothers in charge called a company from town to install some indoor-outdoor carpet on the porch. They did the job Saturday morning, and the guests arrived about 1:00 PM. My lesson: you can work when it is time to work, rest when it is time to rest, play when it is time to play, and put your heart and mind fully into whatever you are about at the moment. To not have to make a decision at every turn is to have the freedom to experience every event to the fullest.

The consistent rhythm of the monastery gave me a very new and different experience, one that when carried into life outside the monastery, with whatever modifications were necessary, became very valuable. It taught me something about why God put structure and rhythm into the natural order of things. We were made to operate within that structure and rhythm, and we ignore it at our own peril. To disregard the structure is to diminish life, even while it seems as if life is offering (or demanding!) more and more. True freedom is found best within structure, and that contributes to life very positively.

Then, the first thing to slowly disappear in a life of frenetic activity is God Himself. The rhythm of the Sabbath was given to us in part to keep that from happening.

Sabbath and Rhythm

Rhythm is a great necessity in and of itself, but God also ordered some specific experiences to be a part of that rhythm; thus He instituted the Sabbath. Leave Sabbath out of our rhythm and we are the losers for it, and we rob God of precious time He longs to spend with us.

In *The Rest of God: Restoring Your Soul by Restoring Sabbath*, Mark Buchanan suggests, "Sabbath is both a day and an attitude to nurture ... stillness. It is both time on a calendar and a disposition of the heart. It is a day we enter, but just as much a way we see. Sabbath imparts the rest of God—actual physical, mental, spiritual rest, but also the *rest* of God—the things of God's nature and presence we miss in our busyness" (2006, 3). Sabbath is about ceasing from the normal and paying special attention to the person and presence of God. Both of these things are life-giving. Ignoring Sabbath is to let life drain out of you.

To omit Sabbath from life is also at times to invite physical illness. The body wears down, and the mind becomes weary. It is more difficult to put your heart into anything, and when the crazy frenetic busyness that comes from a total investment required by those who are called to live out the life of Jesus for others finally stops, how often do we find ourselves sick? Sometimes it takes the sickness to actually slow us down, but then some of us even plough through like martyrs and carry on rather than care for our own bodies, minds, and souls.

Sabbath is necessary, and a rhythm is the way to keep it in our lives. God creates us to imitate Him, including a rest on the seventh day, and in the fourth commandment He commands us to rest. It seems to be a big deal to Him! And while it is pointless here to argue particulars of days and habits on the Sabbath (most of which just get us tied up in legalism and therefore transform us once again into slaves), the clear point is that we as teachers need rest, we need it with regularity, and in rest we find unusual opportunity to fellowship with and become intimate with God.

One of the major reasons we need this rest is to keep us from going back to Egypt (Buchanan 2006). We are no longer slaves who are forced to work all day, every day. We do not live under the rule of cruel taskmasters. Jesus set us free from that. But the busier we get and the more we have to accomplish, the more our lives become like the slaves in Egypt—we are required to make more bricks with fewer materials. (Does this not sound like a teacher's life sometimes?) The bricks represent whatever it is we think we must accomplish, and the materials are not just our exterior resources; they are also our internal ones.

It is true that the state and the administration and the parents are sometimes the taskmasters. The more concerned the nation becomes about the state of education in our country, the more bricks they expect teachers to produce, and often with fewer resources. Worse yet, they see resources only in terms of money and physical facilities. There is little or no concern for the soul of the teachers whom they expect to make the bricks. Seldom have I seen school boards that are highly concerned about the personal well-being of their teachers. Yes, the external forces can be harsh taskmasters.

However, we sometimes become our own harsh taskmasters as well. Though external demands are many, those never go as deep as our internal demands to perform and succeed. Funny (hardly!), we live like hired servants and then become our own harshest taskmasters. As Christians we realize that the kingdom work will be hard. We know it takes sacrifice. We know that the cost of following Jesus in our work is going to be high. Combine that with living in a world that values success above all else and there will be Christian slaves—and not slaves to Jesus, but slaves to His work. How easy it is for committed Christians to develop messianic complexes. Yet how far that takes us from God Himself because we have so little time to grow our love for Him—we are too busy doing His work. Nothing about that would resemble being what God made us to be.

Realizing That Sabbath Is Not All There Is to It

Life is experienced as an interwoven whole, yet there are different threads, or categories of life, that need to be recognized and properly managed in our look at rhythm. Robert Benson, in *A Good Life: Benedict's Guide to Everyday Joy* (2004) considers the Rule of St. Benedict for life today and says the four major categories of life are prayer, rest, community, and work. He emphasizes a need for balance in the energy, time, and attention we give to all above.

Balance feels like an elusive experience to me. I don't know many who can keep life balanced, or who even necessarily know what the balance is supposed to look like. More realistically it seems to me that life often comes in waves, and for a given season we often find ourselves giving huge amounts of time and energy to the tsunami that is washing over us. When that wave subsides we will likely have another that comes with demanding force. Sometimes when our children are sick, they take enormous amounts of time and energy away from everything else. Reporting progress on report cards (or whatever means used) takes precedence over almost everything else four or six or however many times in the school year. When a physical or emotional disaster strikes my neighbor, it consumes great amounts of time and energy, both external and internal energy. I am not sure we can escape that, or even that we are supposed to try.

Rather, it seems that a firm but flexible rhythm is a help in dealing with the waves. That rhythm will begin to develop as we first ask ourselves the fundamental question: "Who has God made me to be, and what does it mean to live faithfully to that?" If I believe that I bring glory to God by fulfilling my basic calling to be what He made me to be (that is what we are all called to do), then the things I should give myself to are the things that enable me to be what I was created to be. That should affect decisions about what the major categories of my life will entail.

Yes, the major categories may be prayer, rest, community, and work (though there are other potentially helpful ways to define categories of life), but our discernment about how much of each, and in what priority and in what manifestation, should be based on who we have concluded that God made us to be.

For some teachers that could even mean leaving the profession. For others it could determine what they are willing to put the most energy into as they encourage their students to learn. For some it may mean that they must find ways to "play" as a part of their work. For some it could lead to a different perspective on and practice of evaluating learning, one that utilizes more of who the teacher is and less of what the traditions are.

So what would be the keys to developing a rule, or rhythm, of life? In *Sacred Rhythms: Arranging Our Lives for Spiritual Transformation*, Ruth Haley Barton (2006) gives us good counsel. She says that such a rule or rhythm must first be "very *personal*" (148). It needs to take into account your personality, your spiritual type, your season of life, the sin patterns of your life, and the places you already know God is growing you.

Second, it needs to be "ruthlessly *realistic*" (Barton 2006, 149). Circumstances in our lives change dramatically over the years. To design a rhythm that is unrealistic for your stage and circumstances in life is to ensure defeat at the starting gate.

Third, she says it must be "*balanced*" among those disciplines and life concerns that come easily to you and those that stretch you (Barton 2006, 149). This is particularly relevant for including those dimensions of life that either require you to be alone or those that require you to be in community. Most will find one preferable to the other, but neither can be exclusive of the other.

Finally, she says it must be very *flexible*—deeply intentional but not so rigid that it begins to deny the reality of life: a strong rope but held with a loose grip and a good fence with some gates (Barton 2006, 150). This is extraordinarily important because though a main underlying purpose of the rhythm is to bring a predictability that sets us free to engage fully, at the same time we recognize the complete supernatural unpredictability of God. At any moment He can, and will, bring our way something that completely blows our plans. These things provide us with the opportunity to prove that even though we rely on and function better with a plan, we so completely trust Him that we can set the plan aside at any given time and follow Him into a dark room, without a flashlight because we know He can see in the dark. We have freedom because of structure, and freedom within structure—even freedom to go outside that structure in order to follow God.

Establishing a Rhythm

In establishing a rhythm for life, it is important to *take stock of your life*. The more you know about yourself, your internal taskmaster, and the circumstances that become external taskmasters, the more realistic and helpful your plan for establishing a rhythm will become. You will need to let your life speak about who you really are. You will need to have special time alone with God to hear what He says about who you are. You may need input from other trusted friends to help you examine the tenor, tone, and rhythm (or lack thereof) of your historical life. You will also need to get some clear snapshots of your current life.

Then, it is important for you to examine *your deepest desires*. God will again need to help you with this. After you have a handle on what God made you to be, you should be able to say something about what you desire to be. Your desires are an absolute necessity for your rhythm of life to be more than simply a time management scheme.

In light of your understanding of yourself and your desires, take a look at *what dimensions of your life may require the most attention*. Experiences or habits that will address those spots in your life should receive high priority in your plan for the rhythm.

However, a rhythm that is designed solely to address weakness will eventually become self-defeating. Therefore, of equally high priority would be those experiences or habits that most readily allow and *encourage you to fly*! We have lost the art of celebration, particularly celebration of who we are as God made us. To fully engage in that which allows us to be who we are is to celebrate with God His workmanship in making us. The rhythm must allow for you to live out who you are, not just be designed to help you get your work done.

To begin, map out a possible rhythm (times and events or tasks) that in some measure aligns with the conclusions you have arrived at from the examinations above. It may be daily, weekly, monthly, quarterly, annually, or whatever time frame suits your life. Eventually you would probably benefit from doing all of these, but initially that could be overwhelming. So start with what you can.

Then, find a trusted friend or group of friends who will walk with you as you begin the journey, not someone to act as the police, but someone who will listen, encourage, ask the right questions, pick you up when you feel like you are failing, and be a real partner for you. Doing this alone is very difficult, and it is not part of God's intended design.

In our day this will also require that you include time in your plan to "unplug." The reflection above certainly will require you to be set apart from distractions. But technology has become such a slave driver, or taskmaster, that your rhythm itself must include time to be unplugged from technology. Being constantly accessible will keep you from ever being able to establish any rhythm. Someone will *always* want you, and the multiple tasks you have not yet accomplished will *always* beckon.

Now What?

What is the rhythm of your life like now? What practices discussed in this chapter might help you in this important realm, and what could you do about them?

17 You Cannot Go It Alone

Because God created us in His image, we are necessarily designed to be in fellowship with others. He also declared that even in a perfect world it was not good for Adam to be alone, and He gave him a helper who was like himself. Loneliness was the first thing God's eyes saw that He declared to be "not good." Even the Lone Ranger had a sidekick. So, the journey into significant change in one's life should never be entered alone. That would apply to teachers who are moving in new directions such as you have been asked to consider thus far.

The Suffering of Loneliness

Loneliness brings suffering. Being alone is not exactly the same as loneliness, since being alone with God is a good thing, and there are many times when we must be alone to look inward to find God. But loneliness is a different matter.

Loneliness implies a time when you are supposed to be with someone else but are not. It suggests that there is no one to be found. It is experienced when you need someone to be by your side or to be with you as you enter a new place or thought and you do not have anyone. Loneliness makes the heart sick and downtrodden. It is just completely unnatural; it is not the way things are supposed to be.

Loneliness can occur in all kinds of circumstances. It may be when something very important has just happened to you and there is no one to celebrate with you. It may occur when you have a terribly difficult task with which you need help and you can't find any. It could arise when disaster strikes and there is no one there to share the grief with you. Or, it can even happen in your profession. Promoting the idea of grace as applicable to school has often been a lonely road for me personally. When over a long period of time, you cannot find anyone who shares your ideas, it can get very lonely.

Dealing with a room full of difficult children can also be a very lonely task. And while teachers are supposed to have backup support, often they do not feel it much. One teacher has even reported to me that when she tries to extend grace to a particular student, other teachers sometimes step in and overrule her, normally making the student feel like a piece of trash in the process. Or, there are reports of a teacher at her wit's end with a student, and after a trip to the principal's office the word simply comes back for the teacher to "deal with it." Teachers who work with marginalized kids from hard places know what it is to be lonely.

The Need for a Safe Place

All human beings need a safe place, as that is what we were created for. The Garden of Eden is the perfect first example; heaven is the next. In between we live in a world that is not safe yet is being redeemed. Being in the middle of that process is a challenge for those of us who work in a school that may be hostile toward our faith, or at best indifferent. Yet if we are to be witnesses to the kingdom as Jesus sent us to be, we must find ways to live and thrive in such places where we are daily confronted with opposition.

Our only true safe place is with Jesus, yet He said we would taste of that and know it through finding safe places with other human beings. To know you are safe with another human being is to know you are safe with Jesus. Thus it is incredibly important that Christian teachers who are in such a minority in public schools find one another and create a safe place for one another.

What does a safe place look like and feel like? First and foremost it means you are warmly welcomed and received just as you are. The only person you are allowed to bring to this place is the real you, sometimes the broken and bruised you, sometimes the joyful successful you, and sometimes the totally confused you. Whatever you bring, you will be received with open arms and heart.

In a true safe place, you will not only not be judged, but you will be delighted in. Because the true you is known, even when there is muck and mud and failure all over you, the one receiving you knows what is real, and it is one in whom the Spirit of Christ dwells. Thus, in a safe place you always feel that the others are so very glad you are there and so glad to know the real you.

You also will not find yourself often corrected and instructed. There are certainly times when the Holy Spirit might speak to you through the mouth of another, but most often He wants you to go down inside yourself to meet Him where He lives and He will talk with you personally there. Other people in your safe place will eventually learn that it is their place to listen to you and then ask questions that will open the door to the room where the Spirit is waiting for you. They help you feel safe enough to listen to what He may have to say.

Finally, a safe place is a shelter for you. It provides refreshment, an opportunity to rest, and healing. You will leave knowing that you have been received and loved and that you are welcome to come back at any time.

Every teacher needs some comrades who can provide a safe place, for the schoolroom is a very challenging place. Some days you must expend all the inner strength you possess to simply get through the day. Regular visits to the safe place are needed to replenish the soul, energize the body, and restart the mind.

Brokenness Leads to Community

There is a great deal of discussion these days about *community*. Everyone seems to recognize the value of it, but it is difficult to define and even harder to know how to create it. But all the buzz means it must be quite important.

Nearly every true community I have been a part of did not arise out of an attempt to build community. Rather, it almost always arose from shared brokenness. A church group that I once helped lead came around a couple who had fallen into infidelity, and after the affected couple shared their brokenness, the group simply could never break up. One form of brokenness led to the confession of others for various, serious forms of brokenness, and we were superglued together. We also stopped trying to fix one another. We wept together, prayed together, and ministered to one another, but we were set free from thinking we had to straighten anyone out or solve his or her problems. It was probably the safest place I have ever experienced.

Brokenness has led to some of the very best relationships I had with students as well. That is true whether we are talking about individuals or groups. One day I shared with a class about my own brokenness over the effects of bad choices made by some students. I was shaken enough that I did not know if I could teach that day. So, I told the class that and asked them to have a prayer meeting for me right there. When we finished a young lady with tears streaming down her face got up and left the room. After class I asked if I had offended her in any way, and she assured me that was not the case. She had just never had a teacher who had been that vulnerable with students before, and it got to her heart. Not long after she came to me with her own brokenness over a painful divorce her parents were about to go through. Twenty years later, with almost all of them spent many, many miles apart, we are still the dearest of friends.

In my years of teaching in a high school, I often found myself developing close relationships with students who lived out on the edge and who were often a real bother to some teachers in the school. The only reason I could ever figure out why was that I felt compelled to provide a safe enough place for their brokenness to show through, and even if I had to discipline them in some fashion, they knew that their broken hearts had somehow captured mine. We experienced community.

Shared brokenness, when the broken people are received and loved, creates a safe place and diminishes loneliness. Broken people can move forward together.

Unity, Diversity, and Adversity in Creating Community

One of the very best experiences of community I have experienced in my teaching career came during a period of involvement with several other faculty members in the teacher education department at the college where I taught. In my earliest years I was the sole teaching faculty member in that department for a year. It was very lonely. But then the Lord began to bring others to the department who proved to be a blessed and wonderful community for me. Here we were not brought together so much by brokenness but by the pursuit of a common goal and a period of great adversity.

In personality, temperament, teaching styles, and fields of expertise, we were about as diverse as we could be. Yet we all pursued the goal of enabling our teacher education students to know what it meant for them to teach "Christianly" in whatever setting they might find themselves. We also had a great appreciation for one another's gifts and talents, and none of us took ourselves too seriously. It was a most pleasant environment in which to work.

We also had the opportunity to build a graduate program for teachers and administrators already in the field. This gave us a common task to which we were committed, but for which we were suited in very different ways. It is a beautiful thing to be able to build something from the ground up, to know that it is a wonderful expression of the things you most deeply believe in, and to know that it took very diverse people with very diverse gifts to build that beautiful thing.

But then adversity struck like a tornado. A preliminary accrediting committee (one with no power) visited us and applauded our very unique program. The next committee (which *did* have power) did all but crucify us. They simply could not wrap their minds around what we were doing, and they felt this program had no business being accredited.

What ensued could only be likened to the story of Jehoshaphat in 2 Chronicles 20 in which the Israelites were about to be annihilated by three huge opposing armies. Jehoshaphat and the people knew not what to do except go before the Lord and wait. As they went out to battle the next morning singing praises to God, they discovered that the opposing armies had completely destroyed one another. This was the fitting picture for our eventual interaction with the accrediting body, who gave green lights to the program in all respects.

Teachers who find themselves in public schools where there is opposition have plenty of adversity. There is also a good deal of diversity among different schools and even among the different Christian teachers in the same school building. When they come together to face a common foe, to pursue a common dream, to implement a common idea, or even just to support one another in any way they can, the air is ripe for community—something God dearly wants us to have.

Soul Friends

"We need someone who encourages us when we are tempted to give it all up, to forget it all, to just walk away in despair. We need someone who discourages us when we move too rashly in unclear directions or hurry proudly to a nebulous goal. We need someone who can suggest to us when to read and when to be silent, which words to reflect upon and what to do when silence creates much fear and little peace," advises Henri Nouwen in *Reaching Out: The Three Movements of the Spiritual Life* (Hernandez 2008, 20).

Soul friends are special kinds of friends, and it may not be that a Christian teacher will necessarily find them among fellow Christian teachers in his or her school or other nearby schools. They may be found anywhere, but what is special about them is that they have a keen sensitivity to the presence of the Holy Spirit in their own life and yours. When they listen to you, they are also listening to the Spirit. They have the ability to ask you questions that open you more to God Himself.

Above all other people, with them you know you are safe. No struggle or failure will shock them or turn them away. No confession will cause them to turn away. Nor will they tell you what you need to do to right the wrong or solve the problem. They help you stay on the path toward God, and they actually make the journey with you.

The ancient Celts had a name for these kind of friends—*anam cara*. They believed that no one dare afford to try to go through life without at least one soul friend. To do so was to be like a body without a head.

Teachers, like all other people, need soul friends. With the demands of teaching, the added demands of difficult students, the added expectations of state and federal government, the woe of an unsupportive administrator, and your own struggles in life always upon you, it may be wise to follow the advice of the Celts. Ask the Lord to provide you with a soul friend or two.

Seeing God in Others

Another value of not going it alone is that you have the blessing of being with other Christians in whom you can see and be blessed by the face of God. Mother Teresa could see the face of Jesus in the dying leper lying in the street, and that is something we can do as well—even in the faces of the most troublesome students. But to see the face of God in another whom you know trusts Him and walks with Him closely leaves you with an experience a bit like that of Moses. When he went into the tent of meeting to be with God, he came out with a face that shone so brightly it had to be covered with a veil.

None of our friends or colleagues would shine so brightly as to require that, but being around someone who is close to God allows you to get close to God. And getting close to God is what will rejuvenate you. Henri Nouwen said that the only thing that changes us is being in the presence of God, and being in the presence of another who is close to God is one way of being present with Him ourselves.

Seeing God in the person of someone you trust and love will also make it easier to become more like Mother Teresa; you may begin to see the face of Jesus in the students who come to your class, even the ones who bring such grief to you. This contributes to seeing them all as image bearers of God, one of the key themes of this whole book. And when that person sees God in you and you know it, you can also see God in others a bit more easily.

You cannot do any of these things or be blessed and renewed by any of them if you have to go it alone. Find someone who can see the face of God in you, and you will be able to see it in others.

Fostering Hope

Ultimately we must hope in God. But as in all other dimensions of life, in His mercy He chooses to give us earthly, tangible sources of hope to point us to the divine hope. There seems to be little in life that encourages us more than being with someone who "gets" us. When someone understands, feels with you, experiences what you experience, there indeed is comfort but also *hope*. That can help you keep going when you might be tempted to give up.

Knowing there are partners who are on the journey with you can also help reduce fear. Fear pushes hope so far away that you sometimes cannot even see it.

Particularly when you face battles, being in them with those who get you and who are with you allows you to hope because you don't need to be so afraid.

Loneliness brings despair. Togetherness brings hope.

Now What?

What community of support do you have to help you respond to the challenges of this book? Where do you need that community to assist you? Or, if you have no such community, where and how could you begin to create one?

Part 6

Responding: Alone and Together

18 Moving Ahead

Bringing the grace of the gospel to bear on all you do in the classroom is a significant challenge. I trust that by now you may have begun to look at teaching a bit differently—at least in some areas of classroom life. Responding to that challenge may indeed seem overwhelming. Perhaps rightly so, for living out the gospel in any part of life is rather overwhelming. Following Jesus anywhere is a bit like standing at the side of a major highway with sixteen lanes of traffic flowing in both directions at seventy miles per hour and hearing Jesus say to you, "Let's walk across the highway to the other side." The task that flows from the vision of this book can be daunting.

If you have come to accept the vision of this book and the beliefs that shape that vision, it is my desire to assist you in the process of implementing what you have read. I don't want this book to become simply a good (or bad) read. I want it to help you make a difference in the way you work with students. Thus, our final chapters will encourage and enable you to do the following:

1. Examine your personal life and relationship to God.
2. Examine your classroom practices in light of the whole book.
3. Proceed through the transitions necessary to implement the changes you desire to make, in both your personal life and your classroom life.

Part of that will happen through your own self-examination and creative, redemptive planning. But it is difficult to change by yourself, especially when the prevailing policies and practices run at right angles to, or perhaps even in contradiction to, what you believe and want to live by. So a part of your move forward needs to be accomplished together with others.

God created us to live and work in community and not just as isolated individuals. Thus, the final chapter will include some thoughts on how you might become partners with your colleagues to begin to implement some of these ideas together. These last chapters are not intended to become a how-to manual though. Use the ideas to guide you, but do not let them rule you.

Let's begin with some questions you can ask yourself about your personal life.

Examining Your Personal Life

- How would I characterize my "walk" with God? Is it truly intimate, or is it not as close as I would like? What do I wish it were like?
- How did I get to where I am right now? Who, and what, influenced and shaped me and my relationship with God—for good or for ill?
- How large is the gap between my head and my heart? What makes me say that?
- There have been peaks and valleys in my walk with God, times when I was very close and times when I felt very distant. Describe those times and identify anything that you feel might have contributed to what you were experiencing at the time.
- How would I describe my prayer life? Does it consist mainly of asking and thanking God for things? Do I have "conversations" with God in which I *listen* as well as speak? Have I ever considered silence to be a part of prayer?
- How is the grace of Jesus so *radical* (remember, this means "thoroughly defining, the essence") in my life? Or how is it not? Do you have an explanation for what you describe that would be helpful to you?
- Do I rest easily and completely in the love of the Father? Could I really call my relationship with Him *intimate*? (The presence of fear in my life reveals a great deal about how much I know His love, for the Bible tells me that fear and love cannot coexist; perfect love, God's love, drives out fear.) How has my relationship to my earthly father shaped my experience with my heavenly Father?
- What do I really know about fellowship (partnership) with the Holy Spirit? Have I ever thought of my relationship with Him in terms of a *dance*? Do I really see Him as a partner in my work? And have I ever conceived of Him as the one leading me to rest? Comment on some of these things.
- How have I (or have I not) viewed my students and myself as image bearers of God? What difference has that made in the way I do things in the classroom and out?

- How have I allowed (or not allowed) grace to become the atmosphere of my classroom? How much of my interaction with students still seems based on law?

Not Walking Alone

While the kind of questions above will require a good bit of personal soul-searching, the territory to which that might lead you is not a place you should go alone. You need some traveling partners—people to whom you can entrust yourself as you make the journey. As you consider trusting yourself to others, and their trusting themselves to you, it is important that you consider both the *people* with whom you might journey and the *practices* in which you engage one another. Both are important.

The people. If you enjoy working together with others, it is tempting to jump quickly to those people you already know and with whom you are comfortable. You might likely go to your good friends. I want to suggest that you not move in a hurry but rather that you begin in prayer, asking the Lord to lead you to, and open your eyes and heart to, people He might have accompany you on your journey. He sometimes has a surprise in store for us.

I would encourage you to find two other people with whom you can commit to work and share your lives and experiences over the course of the year. You will form a triad that is meant to become a safe place for you as you continue. These should be people you do feel you can trust, who you think may have insights that would help you, and ones you think you would be willing to give yourself to in ways that might support them. It is not necessary that these people be like you or even think like you. It is necessary that you come to believe that the Lord has orchestrated the makeup of the triad though. These people will constitute a small "circle of trust" for you—a term borrowed from Parker Palmer (2004).

These people may or may not be your colleagues at school. If they are, they may also become the working triad for your attempts to implement the teaching concepts in the book (to be described in the final chapter). But they do not need to be colleagues from your school, and for this part of your journey you may prefer that they not be. That is entirely up to you. It may even be possible for you to link up with folks who are at some distance, using the technological capabilities currently available. I just don't want you to go on this adventure alone.

The practices. The name *circle of trust* is appropriate, for together you will become a place where it is safe to explore and share your journeys toward intimacy with God and where you can trust and be trusted to enter into one another's lives rather than trying to fix or save one another. Circles of trust are not therapy groups. They are not study groups. They are not confessionals. They are meant to allow and encourage all participants to explore their relationship to God with people who are on the same journey and who can ask questions and offer reflections that may help each person hear more clearly from God.

As your self-selected group forms, you need to set some parameters. I would suggest some of the following, but you are in charge and you should decide:

- Select a place (either physically or electronically) where you can meet that is comfortable and inviting and where you will not be interrupted or distracted.
- Meet once a month for whatever time period is workable—I would suggest an hour to an hour and a half.
- See yourselves as coleaders, equally in charge.
- Decide on a format to follow for sharing your stories, for that will be much of what this is about. You may decide to focus on one person each month, or you may decide to split the time so all three get some focus time at each meeting. The point is that everyone needs to have the opportunity to tell the story of his or her own journey with God.

As you share your stories, there are a few ground rules:

- All that is said must be kept *completely confidential* unless someone voluntarily reveals something that could be very harmful to self or another. Your time should not be discussed with other colleagues or even spouses.
- You are there to *listen and enter into one another's stories*. Silence is a good thing, and sometimes it should not be broken.
- You may *ask questions that will help clarify something* for you or for the person sharing the story, but you *may not attempt to advise, fix, correct, or instruct* one another as you respond. If things begin to go in that direction, the third person in the triad is responsible for stepping in to stop it.

What will you talk about? I would suggest that you begin with time to share how you feel about doing this. Then, I would suggest that you each share (in whatever format you have chosen) the things that have been revealed to you in your self-examination questions. That will be an ongoing process. Telling the story may be the easy part; responding to the stories of the others will be harder. Appropriate types of responses follow:

- Ask, "How are you experiencing God in all this?"
- Say, "Here are ways I see God revealing Himself and His character in you as I listen to your story."
- Say, "Your journey reminds me of this event, character, or situation in the Bible."

- Ask questions that are designed to allow those sharing to clarify their thinking and to go deeper into themselves to find God.
- Be silent.
- Say a prayer that invites God to take the storyteller deeper into his or her true self and to give the storyteller what it takes to be willing to go there. Pray that God will continue to make Himself known to the storyteller as well.

Finally, twice a year use one of your sessions to step back and evaluate what has been happening in the group, with an eye toward what, if anything, may need to be changed. You do not need to keep on with something that is not helpful.

Examining Your Classroom

Things you are doing that are consistent with what you have read. First, examine your teaching practices in the area you have selected in light of what you have read in this book. Undoubtedly, you will recognize certain ideas that already characterize you as a teacher. Begin by identifying your practices that seem to illustrate the ideas presented in the book and that seem to carry out the implications of those ideas as described here. Be fairly specific in your description.

Where has your teaching been inconsistent with what you have read? As you consider the differences in your practice and the ideas espoused in this book, you may see both good and bad reasons for those inconsistencies. Begin with what you feel are good and justifiable reasons for the differences. Be careful not to justify yourself too quickly and without serious thought, but do not be afraid to differ with me for good reason. After all, one book could never cover everything in regard to teaching, and I hope the time never comes when I believe my ideas are beyond challenge and question.

Next, identify some practices in your teaching that have not lived up to the ideas expressed in this book. Which practices lack something, which are misguided, or which are somehow not as they should be in light of what you have read? This examination is perhaps the most important to you, since it could create the necessary tension for you to grow. Be honest, and don't be afraid. Just as the conviction of sin is the first step to forgiveness and freedom to live righteously, so conviction of failure to live up to some ideals might be the first step in making your teaching more consistently Christian.

As you identify practices that are not up to par, think carefully about why they are not. You are not likely to change your practices if you do not deal with the underlying reasons that have led you to do what you already do. The following questions might help you in your thinking:

- Had you just never thought about it this way?
- Is it contrary to your training and experience as a teacher?

- Are you afraid that you might lose control or that it might not work?
- Have you been directed to do it another way by some authority?
- Do you think your peers, perhaps your students, and especially the parents of your students might resist an approach that is more redemptive in character?
- Do you lack knowledge or skill?
- Do you generally resist change or avoid risks?

Now What?

The self-examination asked for here is rather daunting. How can you proceed, and who do you want to take the journey with you?

19 | Implementing Changes in Your Classroom

Planning for Change

What you might do differently. As you consider what you might do differently, do not be afraid to think somewhat radically at first. Try not to let your mind be shackled by thoughts that "it will never work, my principal will never let me do that, or my students will refuse to participate." You may be right, but you will never be able to think creatively if you let these barriers paralyze you at the outset. And you will never change anything if you give up before you try. Later in the process, you will need to think about opposition and difficulties that might prevent you from successfully implementing your ideas, but do not "cut off your own leg" at this point.

Select a particular class, subject area, topic, student, group of students, or whatever real-life situation you wish to use as the context for your creative thinking. Describe what you would like to do in your teaching that would more accurately reflect what has been discussed in this book. Again, describe it in some detail, and do not be afraid to step out of your comfort zone.

Resources that you will need to implement your plan. After you have completed a description of what you would like to change, you will need to think about the resources you will need to make the change. I suggest the following kinds of resources, though again I do not wish to limit your thinking:

- Human resources—people who will help you (colleagues, parents, experts, students), who will need to cooperate with you or agree with what you want to do, or who can give you some advice, direction, and support
- Fiscal resources—money you may need to buy materials, to take students to places, or to obtain some additional training
- Physical resources—equipment, places outside the school building
- Curriculum resources—teaching materials, primary source materials, unit guides
- Permission of authorities—if necessary
- Time—for planning (cooperatively or individually), for implementing, for evaluating

Barriers you may face. When you begin to think about implementing a plan for change, you will undoubtedly face some barriers. The barriers may be internal or external, but you need to identify as many as possible so you can face them and deal with them. They may stop you, force you to modify your plan, cause you to change your timetable, and so on, but you can overcome them. If your plans are worth anything, you should desire to do the latter. The following are some possible internal barriers:

- Fear of the unknown
- Fear of failure
- Rigidity or skepticism
- Lack of knowledge or skill
- Lack of confidence

Some possible external barriers include the following:

- Time pressure
- Administrative, parental, or student resistance
- Lack of resources (all the kinds mentioned previously)
- Tradition
- Structure of the school day
- Curriculum guides and teacher manuals
- Expected results on achievement tests

Whatever your personal barriers are, it would be good for you to identify them and write them down.

Planning to overcome those barriers. Once you have identified the potential barriers, you should think creatively about how you can overcome them. My first suggestion is that whenever possible, you should not try to do so by yourself. Our individual thinking is often quite narrow and too dependent on our own previous experience and thought—just what we are trying to change. You should have a group of people help you with the process if at all possible.

Though you are in effect engaged in the problem-solving process already, this is the place in the process where your creativity should flow freely, and the restrictions of logic should be put behind you. I have used the following group problem-solving exercise in my teacher education classes with some success. I include it here merely as an example.

I tell the group a story about Sir Wiggins, a fine dog who has lived his entire life in Lookout Mountain, Georgia, along the Tennessee border. His family has just moved across Chattanooga to Signal Mountain. Unfortunately, they were so caught up in packing and moving that they forgot him. Sir Wiggins must now find his own way to the new home. He will obviously face some difficulties in going through a big city to a new place. But he wants to get there, for when he does he will be able to live again with his family, and his life will have new adventures and new meaning.

I then ask the group to identify five problems that Sir Wiggins might face in finding his new home on Signal Mountain. We list the problems across a large blackboard or individually on sheets of newsprint and post them on the wall. Next I ask the group to brainstorm about how Sir Wiggins could deal with each problem. I encourage them to let their minds fly free—however silly and unrealistic their ideas may be. This is not a time for logic; it is a time for some real fun.

When there is a good list of possibilities for each problem, the group identifies five problems they will face in trying to change their teaching and then in implementing their plans. These problems are placed on the board or on newsprint pages as Sir Wiggins' problems were. The group compares their problems to Wiggins' problems. As they identify a problem of their own with one or more of the dog's, they use their admittedly crazy-looking solutions to Wiggins' problems as springboards for solutions to their own. It is remarkable how many usable ideas may spring from what appears to be mere silliness. These ideas can then become part of the plan to overcome the barriers to more redemptive teaching.

Transitional objects or practices. When we move toward an unknown place in our lives, it is often helpful if we take along transitional objects or practices. They make us feel safer in the new place. Ira, in the children's book *Ira Sleeps Over* (Waber 1975), needs to take his teddy bear with him the first time he spends the night at a friend's house as a young boy. His sister tells him that his friend will laugh at his need to sleep with a teddy bear and that he'd better not take it. His friend is boisterous and energetic, and he seems too grown-up to need teddy bears. Ira wrestles with this dilemma and at first does not take his teddy bear. But as he and his friend get ready for bed, he is very nervous without it. He timidly asks his friend what he thinks about teddy bears, and his friend ignores him. He sheepishly but determinedly goes next door to his house to get his teddy bear and returns to find his friend fast asleep with his own teddy bear. Knowing that, Ira can also go to sleep.

We are a lot like Ira when we face new situations and when we are about to try new teaching ideas. It can be scary to move away from the familiar. So even though our whole point of moving is to leave the familiar, it may be wise and necessary for us to take some objects or practices (teddy bears, if you will) with us to make the transition. Identify some such objects or practices from your previous or current teaching that, if taken with you, would perhaps make the transition to a new method or approach more comfortable.

Implementing the Change

There is certainly no neat formula for implementing change. It helps if you have thought through the process carefully enough and have written a plan. In addition to the ideas presented thus far in this chapter, you will probably need some of the following:

- The steps you will take
- A timetable
- A means of evaluating what is happening as you implement and complete your new effort (A journal would be a helpful part of this process as well as a more formalized way of evaluating the success of your new approach.)
- Someone sympathetic enough to pray and work with you and to help you evaluate what is happening (A colleague would be wonderful, but that may not always be possible.)
- The courage to fail, if it turns out that way, and the commitment and confidence in the Lord's love for you to get up and try again, or to try something else

A Simple Form for Use in Planning

The form used to aid you in this process is very simple and very open. It is provided here in a condensed outline version, and you may expand or modify it to fit your needs.

    I. Self-examination

        A. Practices that are consistent with the redemptive teaching ideas of this book

        B. Practices that are not consistent with the ideas of the book and why they are not

            1. Practices that are justifiably different

            2. Practices that are not so justifiably different

    II. Planning for change

        A. Description of what I/we might do differently

      B. Resources I/we will need

      C. Barriers I/we will face

      D. Ideas for overcoming these barriers

      E. Transitional objects or practices

  III. Implementing the change

      A. Steps I/we will take

      B. Timetable

      C. Means of evaluating the new approach

      D. My support team and what I/we will ask of them/one another

Now What?

The implementation of ideas from the book is even more daunting than the self-examination. How will you proceed, and who will accompany you?

20 Final Considerations

Starting Small

Changing the way you do things in your classroom requires you to let go of some old ways in order to grasp onto new ones. That process is never easy, nor should you expect it to be. Moving into the unknown, especially when you know there are risks involved, can be downright frightening. But joy and fulfillment in teaching come in part through being able to live out what you believe, so as you consider implementing some of the ideas of the book you should begin with some concept that really rings true with you and that you are developing strong convictions about. It will take courage and perseverance to implement change that may disrupt the normal way of doing things.

I would suggest that you choose an idea that has struck you in relation to one of the major themes of the book: relationships, grace as the classroom atmosphere in which to build those relationships, viewing yourself and your students as image bearers of God, caring for your own soul, or community. Then try to connect it with a concern in the realms of curriculum design; learning activities; measurement, evaluation, and grading; or classroom behavior and discipline. It is certainly possible to take an isolated idea from any section of the book, but these are areas where the "rubber hits the road," so to speak. Selection of one of these areas could also affect the establishment of the triads, since members might want to pursue ideas in one particular dimension.

The final thing to consider is that you should begin with very small changes. Most of us cannot deal with sweeping changes because the disruption is just too great. Our students will not deal well with sweeping changes either. If you can find one idea in your area of choice to implement in your teaching each semester, you will do well. Big ships change direction very slowly. As you identify what you want to do differently, state it as clearly and as concisely as possible. Then, you must examine what you are currently doing in relation to that practice.

Working with Others

Assuming (and hoping) that there may be a group of Christian teachers in a public school or nearby schools that is serious about implementing the ideas in this book (a large and important assumption for what follows here), I offer some suggestions as to how you might proceed together. Remember, these are just ideas that come to my mind. It is important that you, as creative image bearers, follow ideas that come to your minds. If my ideas help you get started, fine. If you devise better ones, use them.

If each teacher involved has been doing the individual self-examinations, the results of those examinations can be used as a starting point for the smaller groups that will need to work together. Or a different approach might be for a small group of teachers who teach the same subject area or grade level to decide to work together in one of the four realms for their classes. Teachers should decide for themselves how to best form groups and what new practices or ideas they want to implement.

Though I am not trying to promote book sales, reading this book is an unavoidable prerequisite. Little could be accomplished unless the teachers involved have had exposure to the ideas and time to chew on them.

The year (or semester) could begin with a general discussion of the content, its meaning for your school as a whole, issues that will undoubtedly arise from taking the ideas seriously, concerns and questions you may have, and a reasonable measure of commitment to push forward. In a public school you will likely have to be committed to the idea that you can start with a few teachers who are with you and then see how the changes may ooze into the school milieu. They may or may not, but regardless your classes will be an opportunity for students to grow and change.

The number of colleagues in your school who are interested in the concepts of the book will determine how many groups of teachers there may be, but I would suggest a group size of three if that is possible. Your local circumstances will determine the parameters, however.

Each teacher should decide on an idea to be implemented, and it may even be helpful if teachers do not choose the same idea. Of course, it might be helpful if they did—the choice is again yours. There are advantages and disadvantages to both. As much as seems feasible, each teacher should think through the suggestions in "Implementing the Change" section of the previous chapter.

As any new idea for implementation arises, it is important for all teachers to ask themselves a few questions. The first is "What?—let me make sure I understand what idea is being presented." The second question is "So what?—what would be the implications of this idea for me and my class or students personally?" And third, "Now what?—how should I respond to this idea? What should I do about it?" These are important questions for the teams to discuss as each member develops a plan to implement an idea.

Teams should meet formally once a month and informally as often as they would like. Any way the school administration can be enlisted to facilitate the scheduling of this time together would be wonderful, but I realize that is not always possible in some schools. Some administrators might actually be opposed to the idea, so teachers will have to be creative to make some time to work together on their ideas.

The meetings should provide opportunities for each member of the team to tell the story of what is happening as he or she attempts to implement an idea. It is important that the listeners do not operate as critics and evaluators who try to "instruct" the teacher on how to do things better. As listeners, their role is support, encouragement, and prayer. Listening may require them to step out of the teacher role as they try to support their colleagues. (Let me warn you, this change alone will not be easy. Our lives as teachers have long been defined by telling others what to do, finding right answers, and controlling things in ways that "work." You should know by now that such is not my definition of what teaching is about. Rather, we are trying to draw out of another that which God has placed there in His image. It is very different—and challenging.)

The Center for Teacher Renewal attempts to provide opportunities for ideas and discussions to be shared among Christian teachers around the world. This would hopefully help those who feel quite isolated in their particular school, and it would also become a network of sharing good practices and difficult challenges. (See appendix A for more information.)

Cautions

I want to caution you particularly about dealing with resistance as you attempt to move forward. You may have your own resistance to some of the ideas, but you certainly can expect some initial resistance from students, parents, and even colleagues. Please pay careful attention to the comments in the "Barriers you may face" portion of the "Planning for Change" section discussed earlier. Expect resistance, and respond in accord with healthy ways to overcome it. Some suggestions are given in the "Planning to overcome those barriers" portion of the same section. Perseverance will be a very important part of this when you work in an environment where you know there is opposition to your faith. However, all the things that have been discussed and set forth as challenges here are within the bounds of your legal rights and freedoms.

You also should expect both success and failure. You should expect to modify in midstream. You should expect to feel good and bad about your efforts. You should expect to enjoy your new approach some days and also to question it severely on others. When the Holy Spirit is in charge, you seldom know what to expect. Thus, try to be flexible and trust the Holy Spirit with your emotions and reactions.

Then, I suggest that you accept the fact that moving your classroom ethos toward one that more fully reflects what grace is about is a long-term project. Even thinking in terms of how we *do* school rather than thinking about *what we say* in school is a long-term overhaul. Be patient—with yourself, with your students, with the parents of your students, and with your colleagues.

Finally, remember that you are doing these things because they arise out of your deeply held convictions, not because they are new techniques. If you cannot live out what you believe, life is not worth much. Be true to your convictions and stand by them—even if you have to walk across sixteen lanes of traffic.

Bless you for reading, for thinking, for trying, and for loving your Lord, your students, and what you do.

Now What?

If you can find other teachers in your school (or district) who will join you in this journey, that is wonderful. Be it together or alone (I so hope not!), you are advised to *start small* and *observe certain cautions*. It is possible that the way you have responded to the questions at the end of previous chapters has given you some big visions and ideas. Please begin with the concerns expressed in *only one chapter (or at most in one section)* of the book. Find one place to start and start small. Then add more. *Do not be surprised or put off by setbacks or failures.* Seek ways to live out what you believe, and persevere!

PS Postscript

What Happened to Those Children in Chapter 1?

At the beginning we recognized that one thing all children have in common is that they are broken and they come from broken backgrounds. By now I trust you see that there is another, even more significant, thing they have in common—they are all created in the image of God.

Philip Yancey, in *Soul Survivor: How My Faith Survived the Church*, reports on the life of Robert Coles, a well-known child psychologist and professor at Harvard. "What Robert Coles has been talking about all these years is the inherent dignity of human beings, the image of God that lives in all of us, black or white, educated or illiterate, rich or poor, healthy or sick—the spark that makes mortals immortal. He did not start out believing it. But it was what the children told him, and then the novelists, and then his own research confirmed it. And it is what he is trying to tell the rest of us now" (2001, 116–17). Yancey includes some thoughts by Coles from *The Spiritual Life of Children* (1990):

> Sometimes, as I sit and watch a child struggle to do just the right job of representing God's face, His features, the shape of His head, the cast of His countenance, I think back to my days of working in Dorothy Day's Catholic Worker soup kitchen. One afternoon, after several of us had struggled with a "wino," a "Bowery bum," an angry, cursing, truculent man of fifty or so, with long gray hair, a full, scraggly beard, a huge scar on his right cheek, a mouth

with virtually no teeth, and bloodshot eyes, one of which had a terrible tic, she told us, "For all we know he might be God Himself come here to test us, so let us treat him as an honored guest and look at his face as if it is the most beautiful one we can imagine." (Yancey 2001, 116–17)

As Yancey and Coles have recognized the image of God in all human beings, so have the teachers dealing with the children whose stories were mentioned as we began. In brief, here is what happened as the teachers applied that reality to dealing with these children and as they tried to do it in an atmosphere of grace. As you can imagine, the stories are not complete; they are still very much in process. And, they do not always turn out as wonderfully as we might wish. Such is the nature of dealing with *fallen* image bearers in grace; there is no guarantee they will respond favorably, nor is there any determining of a timetable by which they might. But there is reason for hope if we treat all students, no matter what their behavior or situation, as image bearers of God and extend His grace to them.

Terrence. Terrence's teacher knew that Terrence needed more than behavioral modification techniques to calm his tirades and distressed spirit. His teacher was reminded that one of the image-bearing characteristics that Terrence carried was that of a steward or a caretaker of the creation. So his teacher bought a parakeet for the room and placed Terrence in charge, locating the parakeet's perch right on Terrence's desk. For two months when Terrence continued his outbursts, the parakeet would fly away and create even more disruption. Because the bird would fly away during his outbursts, Terrence began to control his behavior so he could remain in charge. The bird learned to trust Terrence so much that he would perch on his shoulder and eat from his hand. Terrence had problems with his classmates, but when the teacher talked with him about being caretakers of other people as he had become for the parakeet, God eventually did work that led the boy to come to the teacher one afternoon and admit that he had hit another student. Terrence had confessed his wrongdoing to the offended student, asked for forgiveness, made peace with the classmate, and then went on his way, leaving the teacher with "his jaw on the floor."

Sonja. Sonja's teacher and principal watched Sonja slump over her desk for a week. He then talked with her. He told her that he could not imagine what she had been through in the past and what she was going through now. He told her that she was a special creation of God and that God loved her enough to suffer for her and with her. The teacher also shared that his own daughter had been born legally blind in one eye and that life had been so tough for her that she wanted to give up. But she had trusted God's promise and triumphed over her adversity in ways that her father could not do himself. Sonja's mother brought Sonja to school one day soon after and asked what had happened because Sonya seemed like a different person. Since then other teachers have given her extra help and resources, and she continues to make notable progress and grow with her classmates.

LaToya. LaToya is old enough to talk heart to heart with her teacher who simply listens in empathy, tells her how much she loves her, and treats her with dignity, respect, and kindness. LaToya now hugs her, and she is making Bs in the class and doing well, considering what she continues to deal with at home.

Shawn. Shawn had had a very disturbing encounter with the principal. The principal had told him what a troublemaker he was and that he was under constant watch with the expectation he would mess up again in a big way. His teacher talked with him and asked him not to think of what the principal said about him but rather to think about what she thought about him—that he was a great kid; he had worked hard; he was succeeding well; and he was polite, upbeat, and positive. She told him he was a joy to have in her class because that is the way she felt about him. Shawn did not say much in response, but he has returned to his happier, more carefree, hard-working self since that talk.

Sierra. Sierra's teacher again took the time to hear Sierra's story and understand the pain she was going through. The teacher asked a couple of other girls in the class to befriend her if they could. They did, and that has made a big difference. One day when the rest of the class was acting up, Sierra stood and told her classmates (who really do not care about her) that if they could not be quiet and work and respect someone like their teacher who cares about them and their problems then they were a bunch of losers. The teacher thanked her, and Sierra grinned and said, "You are welcome." Sierra is much happier and willing to work hard for this teacher.

Joshua. Joshua's teacher wisely tried to separate what Joshua had control over and what he did not. She saw his potential as an image bearer and that he loved writing. She took him to a writing conference where he could pursue his desires and abilities without the crushing responsibilities and circumstances at home. This was something he could control though home was not. He is learning who he is as a writer, and he is not being so completely defined by what happens at home. A boy who once was a discipline problem has now become someone the teacher can count on to lead his classmates.

Darius. Darius was an actor by nature. His drama sometimes provided outlets for him, not always healthy ones. His teacher decided to start a drama club as an alternative for those who were not adept at sports, and she asked Darius to help her. He took on the responsibility, and he did well with it. There also was a kids' service club at the school in which students visited older folks in an assisted-living situation. Darius at first was hesitant to go, since his grandmother who had lived with them had just passed away. He found it difficult to be around people of that age. But with some coaxing and moving gently into it, he soon developed a strong bond with an older man and woman. He became concerned about the needs of others instead of just his own, and he began to think about what he could do to better his community and what he could give to it.

Maria. Maria's cheating led the teacher to have conversations with Maria's parents. During the conversation the teacher bluntly told Maria's parents that they were seeing that their daughter was flawed—a broken person who makes mistakes. They talked about how Maria apparently needed to receive the approval of others in order to feel OK about herself. That certainly included her parents' approval. Maria and her parents were Christians, so the teacher was able to talk about finding a person's worth in Christ instead of the person's performance. Rather than try to find the perfect discipline to keep Maria from ever cheating again, her parents recognized her sin for what it was. She could be forgiven and treated like a mature person, and the pressure from home could be put into perspective. This has definitely strengthened the relationship between Maria and her teacher and also her parents at home.

Leon. Leon's teacher always gives Leon the opportunity to explain what is going on and what he is feeling when he gets into scuffles with other children. She hears him out and then helps him try to think through what a better response would be. He has come to the point where he can express himself well—not only in terms of what he was feeling at the time but also in his apologies and forgiveness. He recognizes when he is wrong, and he can admit that. He and the boy he punched on the playground were advised that there were many things they would be asked to work together on at school and that they needed to find some common ground to work together and also identify the things they should avoid that tended to make them angry. They sat together for a snack, discussed these things, came up with their lists and moved on— not without any further incident, but much more maturely than before.

Lejou. Lejou's teacher and classmates took seriously what it meant for Lejou to think that his name meant nothing and that he felt like a nobody. So, the other students all wrote about what they thought his name meant, knowing him as they did. Their meanings truly honored him, and for his "name box" he had eighteen different meanings for his name, whereas the others only had one. Another boy came forward and said he had stories about Lejou from the time they were in an after-school care program together. When Lejou was presented with his box, he had been given a whole new picture of himself, and he was a changed boy.

Rick. Rick's teacher was determined not to give up on him. For whatever reason, Rick found himself in a ceramics class in which the teacher was showing students how to throw a pot. Rick thought it looked easy, but it was not. However, he was determined to make something of it, and in a couple of days he had turned out a good-looking pot. Others began to take notice of him and his skills, and he became something of a "teaching assistant" in the ceramics class. This role changed everything for him. He was one of the most broken individuals in the class, who everyone thought could do nothing, but given the opportunity, he actually became a teacher of his peers. While he first never wanted to be in school and he had no plans to graduate, he then became something of a star, and he did not want to leave; he kept looking for ways to stay around the school.

Ryan. Ryan's teacher again refused to give up on Ryan even though he had become violent at times. The teacher believed in Ryan, he was not afraid to discipline him, and he refused to let him be nothing. Eventually Ryan graduated. Several years after graduation his teacher happened to see him in a restaurant where he was a cook. When Ryan saw the teacher, he hugged him and wept, telling the teacher how sorry he was for the way he had behaved and saying he did not understand why the teacher kept putting up with him.

Robbie. Robbie was not without his problems in school, but when the school administrator discovered he was a good skateboarder, she connected him with a man in her church who is a big-time skateboarder. He is now like a dad and a mentor to Ryan. Ryan is now helpful to teachers when other kids are doing something they should not be doing, he is a leader for younger children, and he attends the same church as his mentor, getting there—in the city—all on his own.

Charlie. Charlie's teacher could see that Charlie's lack of language ability was affecting his behavior. Because he had no verbal way to express what he was feeling (he did not know what *angry* meant, for instance), he expressed himself physically when he was angry. When an incident occurred the teacher would ask him to sit down and tell her what he was experiencing. She had a computer on which she recorded his every word because she said his words were important. The more he became able to express himself to his teacher in words, the less he had to bully others. He can now think about what he wants to be and can make decisions that help him become that rather than hurt him and others.

Acacia. Acacia's teacher refuses to get angry at Acacia or yell at her when she acts up. He tells her he knows that she is having a hard time and that her situation is really tough. But he then tells her that her behavior is not acceptable and he needs her to behave correctly. She can either choose to do what he asks or he gives her another choice, one that is not so attractive. The choice is hers, but it is narrowed to two possibilities. Even though she may roll her eyes, she chooses one or the other and moves on. She is not out of the shell of her pain, but she has a growing relationship with the teacher and she is responding better.

In all of these cases, though expressed in various ways, the teachers exhibit the following: they all view their students as image bearers of God and insist on treating them as such, they all have developed a strong personal relationship with their students, they will not give up on them, and they give them grace upon grace.

It is very encouraging to hear these stories of individual teachers building relationships and treating individual children with grace as image bearers of God. But I also have had the privilege of visiting and working with *schools* that approach the whole educational endeavor with these convictions in mind. I will briefly describe two. And while the general atmosphere is different simply because these schools are private schools, the object here is to demonstrate that the principles apply to more than just individual teachers in their classrooms.

The first is an alternative high school operated by a dedicated group of Christian teachers and a single administrator. First, it is important to realize that the teachers and the principal are all on the same page, pursuing the same goal—the transformation of lives that have been troubled in some major fashion. There is definite community exhibited by the staff. The students are part of the community also, however, and they know that in a very definitive way. Such is evidenced by the number of graduates who return on Friday mornings for the brunch that volunteers provide for the students and teachers.

Schools of this sort have more than their share of disciplinary issues to deal with. The perspectives described in chapter 3 are embraced by the entire staff and understood and submitted to by the students. Students do not universally respond well, but because they are treated with the dignity and respect that image bearers of God deserve, for most this approach, over time, brings transformation in their lives.

The curriculum is designed to treat students as agents who are responsible for their own learning. Assignments and syllabi are laid out in advance, but students proceed on their own to complete them. They set their own timetables. It is assumed that they attend the school in order to complete a high school education and receive a diploma, and they will do it on their own initiative or not—it is up to them. They are given all the help they need (there are many volunteer tutors who come to the school), and the evaluation system is defined so that anything less than a B is unacceptable. But they can, and must, try again until they reach that level.

Each student has an "advocate" on the faculty—someone who will look out for the student; who will be a counselor and a source of comfort but also one of accountability; who will keep track of progress; and who will be an advocate with parents, other teachers, or sometimes even the law. Most of the time, advocates will meet individually with their students each week.

This school exists under the radar of most, with very little in the way of financial resources, and it has changed lives for eighteen years. Testimonies given by each of the graduates at the end of the year consistently testify to the difference the school has made in the students' lives—through the relationships with the teachers, the fact that they were believed in and cared for as human beings, and that they were given grace upon grace. It is a place of grace that has received grace from God and then given it to the students who attend—most of whom think of themselves as a part of the family.

The second school is an urban elementary school, again operating out of the same Christian framework and commitment on the part of the faculty and staff. Some of these students come from troubled backgrounds and others from very solid homes. Again, the existence of a sense of community that keeps people very close to one another is overwhelmingly evident. Teachers and students alike trust one another. When conflict arises it is handled openly, honestly, non-judgmentally, with reconciliation always the aim. Students are heard and, in fact, always given an opportunity to get in touch with what is going on inside them as they struggle. As they process that, they then can be freer to move toward the others involved rather than shut them off or seek vengeance.

The phrase *freedom within structure* is heard over and over again. Such has proven to be an excellent part of dealing with the fact that all image bearers are also fallen. The structure—in policy, in schedule, in physical arrangement of things—is emphasized strongly at the beginning of the school year. And as students learn to function within that structure, they become much freer to live and move within that structure. They know the boundaries, and they are then freer to do all manner of delightful things within those boundaries. Freedom within structure is physical, curricular, and behavioral. It is something to behold even very young children making choices that affect their day and then watch them purposefully pursue those choices.

The importance of relationship is profoundly evident here as well. They are relationships based on honesty and courage. It is a safe place—safe to mess up, safe to make up with someone when there has been a break in relationship, and safe to try again. This happens between students and even between students and teachers. Seldom have I seen a place where people are treated like image bearers and expected to treat others the same as I have seen in this school.

Finally, one of the principals I interviewed provided further corroboration of the applicability of these ideas. His school is a public alternative high school, and it is small, fairly rural, and part of a local school district. Most of the students who attend this school are way behind academically, and many have difficult home situations. In fact, the principal told me that at one point he had eight students who were homeless during the year.

While the application of the principles of this book started with the principal and his interactions with a few students, the effect on the students and the principal's urging soon led other teachers to catch the picture. Most of those teachers were not Christian believers, but nevertheless they began to adopt practices that treated students with dignity rather than yelling at them. And they gave them some freedom and responsibility rather than assuming they can do nothing but create trouble. When the students messed up, they were given grace through more and new opportunities to try again. The school record shows that almost none of these students drop out, they stay out of trouble much better than before, and the relationships they develop at the school are very significant to them—in some cases like the family they do not have. Some seek ways to stay at the school as long as possible even when they have completed enough credits to graduate.

In all of these schools, as well as in the individual examples, we see the important themes of this book present and alive—*relationships, grace, image bearing, intimacy with God,* and *community.* Attention to the fourth theme—*intimacy with God*—is absolutely necessary if teachers are to continue beyond a few years. You can go on the strength of your dedication, your gifts and skills, and your willingness to sacrifice for a while, but without experiencing a strong intimacy with God you will eventually either wear out and give up or become cold and mechanical in order to survive. In either case you shrivel up as a person and your students lose out on an opportunity to grow and realize a hope. That is education that leads to *death.*

May the themes of this book and the practices to which they lead bring *life* to you and to your classroom.

A   Appendix A: Center for Teacher Renewal

The Center for Teacher Renewal (CTR) is a nonprofit, support-based ministry designed to enable Christian educators to experience the renewing grace of God for themselves and to enhance their professional abilities to teach in ways that reveal that grace in the classroom. The people we hope to serve are Christian educators who work in any kind of setting—Christian or otherwise—who find themselves facing challenges that sometimes push them to the edge. The emphasis at CTR is on *refreshing souls and revitalizing classrooms.*

The director is Donovan L. Graham, EdD, former high school teacher and counselor and professor of education at Covenant College in Lookout Mountain, Georgia. He is the author of *Teaching Redemptively: Bringing Grace and Truth into Your Classroom* and *Making a Difference: Christian Educators in Public Schools,* and he has been an educator, a counselor, and a spiritual guide since 1965. He and his wife, Wilma, have been providing soul care to students and weary pilgrims for over forty-five years. At CTR they provide opportunity for personal growth in intimacy with God and professional development for all interested educators.

Purpose

The purpose of CTR is to provide personal and professional renewal for Christian educators who work with marginalized students in difficult settings.

Goals

The goals of CTR follow:

- To help educators foster practices, lifestyles, and their relationship with God— enabling them to persist and thrive in difficult, draining school situations
- To help educators apply and demonstrate the grace of the gospel and biblical principles to all aspects of their daily work and interaction with students

Services

- Retreats
  - Personalized individual spiritual renewal retreats—for individuals who seek a deeper intimacy with God, direction in their lives, and a renewal of spirit and hope in their professional work
  - Group retreats—for teachers and administrators, with a focus on redemptive teaching, spiritual renewal, and the strength to continue their ministry in difficult circumstances
- Institutes—one-week residencies followed by a year of application and consultation
  - Redemptive Teaching Institute—for classroom teachers who seek to apply biblical principles and the grace of the gospel to all activities of the classroom
  - Schools of Grace Institute—for school administrators who seek to develop an ethos of grace in their schools
- In-service—workshops and conferences at school sites
- Consulting, coaching, and spiritual guidance—on an individual or school basis

Contact

Donovan L. Graham, Director

Center for Teacher Renewal

5685 Loyola Drive

Colorado Springs, CO 80918

Phone: 719-434-8825

E-mail: teachredemptively@gmail.com

Website: www.teacherrenewal.net

B Appendix B: Christian Educators Association International

Christian Educators Association International (CEAI) is a nonprofit, religious association serving as a membership professional association for Christian educators and support staff in public and private schools. CEAI membership consists of teachers, administrators, and paraprofessionals including any person hired by a school district. In addition, they offer associate membership to parents, pastors, school board members, youth leaders, and others concerned or interested in the education of our children.

CEAI is the only association that provides services including professional liability and job action legal protection specifically for Christians serving in public schools. Many Christians are choosing to join CEAI as an alternative to the secular unions who are supporting antifamily agendas.

Vision

God's love and truth transforming our schools

Mission

To encourage, equip, and empower educators according to biblical principles
- Proclaim God's Word as the source of wisdom and knowledge
- Portray teaching as a God-given calling and ministry

- Promote educational excellence as an expression of Christian commitment
- Preserve our Judeo-Christian heritage and values through education
- Promote the legal rights of Christians in public schools
- Provide a forum on educational issues with a Christian worldview
- Partner with churches, parachurch organizations, educational institutions, and parents
- Provide resources and benefits for educators including professional liability insurance

Membership Benefits

- **Professional liability insurance.** Members receive legal defense and protection for their assets (up to $2 million) when faced with a lawsuit related to their profession.
- **Job action protection.** Members receive help with legal fees in case of job action, demotion, or job transfer.
- **Legal consultation.** CEAI consults with several organizations concerning the various legal problems educators face. These organizations include Liberty Counsel, Alliance Defense Fund, Christian Legal Society, National Legal Foundation, Rutherford Institute, American Center for Law and Justice, and Pacific Justice Institute.
- *Teachers of Vision* **magazine.** Keep abreast of issues affecting Christian educators through *Teachers of Vision*, a national magazine published by CEAI. *Teachers of Vision* spotlights a variety of issues pertinent to the Christian educator such as current Supreme Court action, legislation affecting education, curriculum ideas, tips to legally integrate faith and work, and educational resource materials.
- **Newsletters.** Members receive online newsletters with informative articles and the latest in education news.
- **Museum discount.** Members receive a 50 percent discount on their entrance fee to the Creation Museum.
- **Curriculum and resource materials.** Books, tapes, curriculum, and other resource materials are constantly updated to provide both spiritual and classroom helps for members. CEAI endeavors to develop a national clearinghouse for materials with a Judeo-Christian worldview.
- **Internet resources.** Members can interact with attorneys and network with other members online, post résumés, conduct job searches, sign up to receive daily devotionals, visit the online store, and have access to many other valuable resources.

- **Local seminars.** Teachers are empowered, equipped, and encouraged at local seminars around the country. Educators receive powerful input on how to legally and effectively make an impact on their school culture with their faith. Sharing of successful ideas and creative approaches is an encouragement to all.

- **Prayer network.** Members can call or e-mail CEAI with prayer requests, and they can be linked with other members for prayer support. CEAI will assist members to form prayer groups at their school.

- **Chapters and local networks.** A formal chapter or an informal network may be established right in your own community. Both enable members to meet regularly with teachers, parents, and other Christians who share the same vision and values. Through such interaction, educators are sharpened, and they become more effective for Christ in the classroom.

- **Medical/health consultative services.** Members and family can call 1-866-890-CARE (2273) to receive the support of Lighthouse with Healthcare Solutions at no charge. They are a single-point contact that provides confidential assistance to those struggling with drug and alcohol addictions, eating disorders, anxiety and stress disorders, sexual addictions, gambling, and other life-controlling behaviors.

- **Medical insurance.** If in need of medical insurance, members can purchase the level of coverage needed at great savings.

- **Accidental death and dismemberment insurance.** Members are automatically covered by $25,000 of accidental death and dismemberment insurance when riding on a licensed common carrier, anywhere in the world. This benefit will increase by $2,500 each consecutive year members renew, up to $50,000.

- **Christian worldview voice.** CEAI voices the needs of Christian educators and makes an impact on the educational community and our culture from a Christian worldview through publications, news media, personal contacts, and so on.

- **Networking activities.** CEAI networks with church, parachurch, and educational organizations that share common goals. CEAI endeavors to send a CEAI representative to their conferences and seminars to insure that views of Christian educators are addressed.

- **New Testaments in the classroom.** The distribution of God's Word is an important ministry of CEAI. Every effort is made to place the Scriptures in classrooms as a resource for teachers and students. CEAI makes sets of five or ten New Testaments available to members.

- **Credit union membership.** As a member of CEAI you are entitled to participate in a membership service with the Christian Community Credit

Union. Services include ATMs nationwide, personal checking, loans, and a Visa or MasterCard at a low APR.

- **Staff support.** Staff members are ready to assist you. It only takes a phone call to get advice or information regarding legal or educational issues.
- **Other.** Members can purchase life, auto, and other insurance products at a great savings.

There are many other benefits and discounts in the marketplace from membership with CEAI. However, the greatest benefit is that together we as Christian educators, support staff, parents, and friends of education are afforded an opportunity to reach beyond our local areas of influence. As a member of CEAI, you are provided the opportunity to network with other believers to make an impact on the very fabric of education in this nation. Together we can help spread the Christian worldview in action, speech, and the written word to make an impact on the lives of the youth we serve.

Core Values

- Love
- Biblical knowledge
- Respect
- Integrity
- Prayer
- Patience
- Self-control
- Worship
- Truth
- Unity
- Forgiveness
- Faith
- Servanthood
- Joy
- Professional excellence

Statement of Faith

We believe in
- One God eternally existent in the Father, Son and Holy Spirit
- The Bible as the inspired Word of God
- Christ, the Son of God, His virgin birth, His miracles, His vicarious atoning death for our sins, His bodily resurrection and His return
- The need and reality of spiritual conversion by the Holy Spirit through the death and resurrection of Jesus Christ.
- The ministry of the Holy Spirit Who enables us to live a godly life

Contact

Membership Service Center
PO Box 45610
Westlake, Ohio 44145-0610
Office Phone: 440-250-9566
Toll-free: 888-798-1124
Fax: 440-250-9584
E-mail: info@ceai.org
Website: www.ceai.org

R References

Anderson, Charles W. 1987. *What in the world?* Unpublished manuscript, Covenant College, Lookout Mountain, GA.

Barton, Ruth Haley. 2006. *Sacred rhythms: Arranging our lives for spiritual transformation.* Downers Grove, IL: InterVarsity Press.

Benson, Robert. 2004. *A good life: Benedict's guide to everyday joy.* Brewster, MA: Paraclete Press.

Bridges, Jerry. 1991. *Transforming grace: Living confidently in God's unfailing love.* Colorado Springs, CO: NavPress.

Buchanan, Mark. 2006. *The rest of God: Restoring your soul by restoring Sabbath.* Nashville: W Publishing Group.

Campolo, Anthony, Jr. 1980. *The success fantasy.* Wheaton, IL: Scripture Press, Victor Books.

Coles, Robert. 1990. *The spiritual life of children.* Boston: Houghton Mifflin. Quoted in Yancey 2001, 116–17.

DeJong, Norman. 1977. *Education in the truth.* Nutley, NJ: Presbyterian and Reformed.

Dobson, James. 1974. *Hide or seek.* Old Tappan, NJ: Fleming H. Revell.

Douglas, J. D., ed. 1962. *The new Bible dictionary.* Grand Rapids, MI: Eerdmans.

Federer, William J. 2000. *America's God and country encyclopedia of quotations.* St. Louis: Amerisearch, Inc.

Foster, Richard J. 1992. *Prayer: Finding the heart's true home.* New York: HarperCollins.

Frey, Bradshaw, William Ingram, Thomas E. McWhertor, and William David Romanowski. 1983. *All of life redeemed: Biblical insight for daily obedience.* Jordan Station, Ontario, Canada: Paideia Press.

Hernandez, Wil. 2008. *Henri Nouwen and soul care: A ministry of integration.* Mahwah, NJ: Paulist Press.

Jaarsma, Cornelius. 1961. *Human development, learning and teaching: A Christian approach to educational psychology.* Grand Rapids, MI: Eerdmans.

Keller, W. Phillip. 1970. *A shepherd looks at Psalm 23.* Grand Rapids, MI: Zondervan.

———. 1983. *Lessons from a sheep dog.* Dallas, TX: Word Publishing.

Lindberg, Christine A. 2004. *Oxford American writer's thesaurus,* s.v. "radical." Ed. Erin McKean. New York: Oxford University Press.

Macaulay, Ranald, and Jerram Barrs. 1978. *Being human: The nature of spiritual experience.* Downers Grove, IL: InterVarsity Press.

Mansfield, Stephen. 2001. *God's role in America.* Nashville: American Destiny Press.

Moon, Gary. 2004. *Falling for God: Saying yes to his extravagant proposal.* Colorado Springs, CO: WaterBrook Press.

Nouwen, Henri. 1975. *Reaching Out: The three movements of the spiritual life.* New York: Doubleday. Quoted in Hernandez 2008, 20.

Oxford University Press. 2005. *The new Oxford American dictionary.* 2nd ed., s.v. "radical." New York: Oxford University Press.

Packer, J. I. 1979. *Knowing man.* Exeter, England: Paternoster Press, 1978, *For man's sake.* Repr., Westchester, IL: Cornerstone Books.

Palmer, Parker J. 2004. *A hidden wholeness: The journey toward an undivided life.* San Francisco: Jossey-Bass.

Pelton, Robert W. 2008. *America: A Christian nation? Here are the facts.* West Conshohocken, PA: Infinity.

Pratt, Richard L., Jr. 1979. *Every thought captive: A study manual for the defense of Christian truth.* Phillipsburg, NJ: Presbyterian and Reformed.

Stott, John R. W. 1978. *Christian counter-culture: The message of the Sermon on the Mount.* Downers Grove, IL: InterVarsity Press.

Snyder, Thomas D., and Sally A Dillow. 2011. *Digest of Education Statistics 2010* (NCES 2011-015), Table 42. Washington, DC: National Center for Education Statistics, Institute of Education Sciences, U.S. Department of Education.

VanVonderen, Jeff. 1992. *Families where grace is in place.* Minneapolis, MN: Bethany House.

Waber, Bernard. 1975. *Ira sleeps over.* Boston, MA: Houghton Mifflin.

Walsh, Brian J., and J. Richard Middleton. 1984. *The transforming vision: Shaping a Christian worldview.* Downers Grove, IL: InterVarsity Press.

Yancey, Philip. 2001. *Soul survivor: How my faith survived the church.* New York: Doubleday.